You are going on a journey.

From outer space
to the inner mind.

From the past to the future,
or rather to many futures.

From the imagined realms
in books and movies
to the realities of modern society.

You're already on this journey.
It's called life.
Get better prepared for it.

the MISCosity MANIFESTO

A GUIDE TO FLOWING SMOOTHLY THROUGH AN ULTRA-COMPLEX WORLD

by **CLARK HUMPHREY**
profusely illustrated

SEATTLE USA

Clark Humphrey also wrote:

The Perfect Couple: A Story in 178 Scenes (Eastgate Systems, 1991)
LOSER: The Real Seattle Music Story (1995; revised 2016)*
The Big Book of MISC (1999)*
The Myrtle of Venus (2003)*
Vanishing Seattle (Arcadia Publishing, 2006)
Take Control of Digital TV (TidBITS ebook, 2007)
Seattle's Belltown (Arcadia Publishing, 2007)
Walking Seattle (Adventure/Keen, 2011; revised 2018)
Then & Now: Seattle (Arcadia Publishing, 2011)
Who Am I? Why Am I Here? (2016)*

And contributed to:

Rob Wittig's *Invisible America* (Wesleyan University Press, 1994)

Maire M. Masco's *Desperate Times: The Summer of 1981* (Fluke Press, 2015)

Elaine Bonow's *NOCO Writers in Quarantine* (2021)*

Elaine Bonow's *NOCO 2024* (2024)*

(*available from MISCmedia)

© 2025 Clark Humphrey.
Many illustrations realized via Microsoft Designer and BeFunky.
All quoted text and art © their respective creators and/or publishers.

•

this edition: March 2025

ISBN (this edition): 978-1-929069-03-3

MISCmedia
1901 Western Ave., #104
Seattle WA 98101
miscmedia.com

THE MISCosity MANIFESTO

Why I'm doing this:

The world needs a better way to think. Heck, the world needs TO think. To see. To interact.

And people of all genders and ages etc. need a guide, not to make order of the world (which is impossible), but to live and even thrive amid the chaos.

We don't need to change the world (well, not completely). We need to become better adapted to the world as it really is. And that is what will make for a better life for everyone.

How I came to believe in miscellany,
not as a leisure pursuit but a way of life:

I'd always loved old books, magazines, and other printed "ephemera." In the mid 1980s, my favorite store was a little ephemera shop on Seattle's Capitol Hill. It didn't really have a name, just a series of signs in its front windows. Among the phrases was MISC. ITEMS.

In 1986 I was asked to write a monthly column for a tabloid newspaper run by a tiny arts organization. I chose the title MISC, to express that it would contain a little bit of everything, in the manner of old "three-dot" newspaper columns like that of my local journalistic idol Emmett Watson.

I ended up using the name, or variations of it, on most of my writing and publishing endeavors ever since: a column in the city's top alt-weekly, several print zines, a blog, an email newsletter of local news headlines, a book enterprise.

But "miscellany" became, for me, more than just an excuse to write about all (or most) of the many things I loved to discuss.

It evolved into an overall approach to seeing the world. A way that's guided me all these years.

INTRODUCTION 6

I've been toying with these ideas for several years now.

I had a long-ish draft in 2022, mostly predicated on trying to teach younger people to think how I think (non-linear, high-functioning autistic).

But that approach had its problems. Chief among them: trying to teach people to think how I think would be as futile as the last act of the rock opera *Tommy*. (Teaching people to be "enlightened" in his own way, by blindfolding them and leading them to pinball machines.)

But: The events of late 2024 proved to me that a new way of thinking, relating, being, doing, etc. is still absolutely needed.

Too many people proved to be dangerously trapped in false narratives, false binaries, and false simplicities. In false notions about the world and about humanity, notions that solidify hierarchies of power and wealth.

So, after much cutting and editing, I present to you: MISCosity.

The art of flowing, solidly but smoothly, through a world more complex than we can ever understand.

It's both a vision of the world and a prescription for living in that world.

And as such, it's at least a glimpse of a path toward creating a better world.

Enough of the prelims; let's start at a good starting place: You, and the interface between you and everyone/everything else.

The world's confusions aren't a bug. They're a feature.

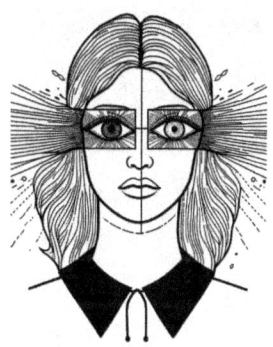

Through the millennia, philosophers, preachers, and orators have said that most of us see the world as a narrower, shallower, simpler place than it is.

A lot of people agree that certain designated capital-O "Others" see the world too shallowly, but fail to recognize this fault among themselves.

At its simplest, this is like urban hipsters stereotyping everyone other than themselves as hicks and "sheeple"; or like white and/or Christian nationalists claiming that other races/religions constitute lesser species.

On a slightly more sophisticated level, this line of thinking includes Plato's allegory of the cave, in which the mass of humanity is compared to someone watching shadows along the wall of a cave and presuming that to be the allegedly "real" world.

I'd say we're all seeing a "shadow world." Yes, even those of us who boast of being learned or enlightened or at least above average.

I, like every human, have limited perception. Our eyes, ears, and other senses have limited "spectra" of sensation.

And our minds, even with the aid of modern science and technology, only know so much about the heavens and the earth, the animals and the plants, the ecosystem outside our bodies and the brain and mind inside them.

Take a moment to ponder the bigness of space, the smallness of molecular biology, and all the other extremes.

We've learned (and in a few cases, learned, forgotten, and then relearned) so much, only to realize how much we still don't know. (Examples: the positions of the sun, moon, and stars; the seasons of the year; weather patterns.)

ARE YOU PONDERING WHAT I'M PONDERING, PINKY?

More pondering:

The earth.

Metals, mining, chemicals, medicines whether "traditional," chemical, or biotech in origin.

Biology, biosystems. Forests, seas, deserts, tundra.

Physics, mechanics.

Math; the "music of the spheres."

How all these are interrelated.

And, of course, this is just the shallowest of surface-skimming.

So: The world, including but not limited to planet Earth, is big and complex.

And our minds are relatively small and simple.

How to respond? For people in some traditions (including the tradition of "individualism," it's with religious or spiritual awe. (A modern variant: the notion that we are living in a "simulation.")

Others, employing the eternal human quest to Explain, have collaborated on developing explanations, some in the form of mythologies, some of those mythologies extremely elaborate. Heavens and hells; angels and demons; gods and goddesses and demigods and enchanted animals and so on. Origin stories for everything.

Early civilizations (just about all of them) tracked the patterns of the sun, moon, stars, seasons, and tides.

They learned to rely on these rhythms for hunting and gathering, then for organized agriculture and sea travel, then for pondering what lies beyond our world.

By 18th-century Europe, some thinkers had come to believe in "the clockwork universe," the notion that everything was ruled by predictable physics like one giant mechanical machine. A universe that always ran according to known, or potentially knowable, rules. Centuries before that (i.e., before mechanical clocks were developed), the Greek mathematician and philosopher Pythagoras talked about "the music of the spheres" (*"musica universalis"*).

It's the notion that the earth, sun, moon, and stars moved in a harmonic, harmonious manner. Everything had an order, one we could use to know when to plant and harvest crops, etc.

"For everything there is a season, and a time for every purpose under heaven."

But there were always exceptions to the way things always went. Fifty-year droughts. Hundred-year floods. Volcanic eruptions. Meteors. Tsunamis, tornadoes, hurricanes, dust storms, crop failures.

People saw early on that the world around them was often as fickle, as ultimately unpredictable, as people themselves were.

The obvious conclusion: the world was being run by super-powered, but emotionally very imperfect, beings.

People developed belief systems in fickle, capricious, superhuman entities: the angry and judgmental Jehovah; the selfish and rapacious Zeus. These people did whatever they believed would appease their godly overseers: prayers, petitions, fasting, sacrifices, temples, artworks, complex rituals of devotion. If unexpected bad things still happened (which they did), at least the worshipers could assure themselves they'd tried.

AN ANTIDOTE TO 'AN ANTIDOTE TO CHAOS'   10

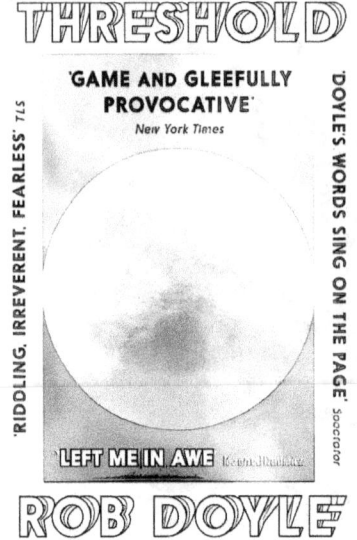

And with capital-E Explanations of the world come Explanations of who and what people are, and how their families and societies should be organized.

Just like many explanations of the larger world (even the really elaborate ones) are too simple (and inaccurate), many explanations of human and societal ideals are also way, way too simple (and inaccurate).

Over-simplified, capital-E Explanations are the root of SO MANY of our problems.

Hate and bigotry are often based on false simplicities and false binaries. Among the many examples of these: Racism, sexism, white supremacy, wars of religion, wars in general, etc.

(Rob Doyle, Threshold): "The ones to be feared and resisted were not the preachers of decline, the diviners of our civilization's exhaustion, but all those wild eyed zealots who strove to create a heaven on earth, refusing to see that, in so doing, they would inevitably unleash hell. Absolutists, zealots, demagogues, jihadists, messianic utopians—all manner of fanatics thrived in the contemporary chaos, exploiting the frightening complexity of the age to hawk their simplistic narratives, their archaic binaries that brooked no ambiguity and sanctioned bottomless bloodshed."

So: Don't seek what Jordan Peterson calls "An Antidote to Chaos."

There isn't any, not really.

In humanity, as well as in the outside world, to quote an old Facebook cliché, "It's Complicated."

Chaos (or at least seeming chaos) is in everything and everyone.

It's in quantum mechanics.

In mathematical distributions.

In games of chance, including life itself.

And it's in human minds, souls, and behaviors. We need to accept it, appreciate it, love it. Even learn from it.

About the greater universe: space, math, chemistry, atomic science, etc.: There is Order behind the seeming Chaos, but there is also Chaos behind the seeming Order.

The more we learn, the more ignorant we realize we are.

In fields of science at least, you can look for Order within the Chaos. And in many cases, you can find it.

But look beyond that level of Order and you'll usually get to another level of chaos beyond that.

And so on and so forth, down to the level of subatomic particles. Which themselves have elements of Order, Chaos, and the hidden Order that seems like Chaos to many human observers.

(Megan Lim, "Why Chaos is Our Greatest Love"): "Without growing pain, there is no measure of progression. Thus, a life without turmoil is a life not lived fully. Let us be that molecule that pushes against the walls to seek foreign territory beyond its container. Let us be that particle that crosses the barrier to the other side. Let us become the definition of entropy. Let chaos become our greatest love."

HOW WEIRD IS IT? 12

Two visions of chaos (or KAOS): The evil enemies of the agents of CONTROL on the classic sitcom Get Smart!; a community radio station in the town of my birth.

(Carl Jung): "In all chaos there is a cosmos, in all disorder a secret order."

(Edward Lorenz' definition of "chaos"): "When the present determines the future, but the approximate present does not approximately determine the future."

•

The best known example of chaos theory may be the "butterfly effect"— the premise that the flapping of a butterfly's wings on one continent can (albeit very indirectly) lead to massive storms on another continent. The storms might seem to have come from nowhere, but they have a discrete rational cause, albeit one our research can't find.

Chaos theory acknowledges the seemingly random. But then it insists there's a perfectly rational cause for everything, even if that cause is beyond our ability to locate it.

But if we don't and can't know the cause of something, it still SEEMS random to us, or at least unpredictable.

So, even if there's no "real" chaos, there's still what I call "effective chaos." Some phenomena look and seem to be random, and we have to know that we'll never know their real causes.

And that's how you have to approach these phenomena, and how you have to approach life itself.

•

THE MISCosity MANIFESTO

My overall term for what I'm talking about here is "MISCosity."

"MISC" as in miscellany.

"-osity" as in viscosity: the thickness and stickiness of a fluid, but also the degree to which a fluid (such as motor oil, maple syrup, or honey) resists "gradual deformation by shear stress or tensile stress." In other words, its resiliency.

The ability to withstand stress while remaining intact: that's the key to human survival, in just about any situation.

To be solid yet fluid, to stay true to your real self as you flow through this strange thing called life on Earth.

The solidity, the viscosity, the fluidity, and the superfluidity (the absence of viscosity) and the superfluity (excess). The underlying chaos, the weirdness.

(Rudyard Kipling, "If—"): "If you can keep your head when all about you are losing theirs and blaming it on you,
If you can trust yourself when all men doubt you, but make allowance for their doubting too..."

**Everything is weirder
and more complex
than our minds can imagine.**

Examples of thick fluids that abound in 'richness' and keep things moving.

MORE DADA, LESS DATA

But everyone can learn to see a little wider, think a little bigger, care a whole lot more.

MISCosity involves understanding the importance of staying solid yet fluid, as you move through a world more complex than you'll ever know.

And this is the path, or at least one path, toward a real-world version of what some call "enlightenment."

Enlightenment is for everyone, not just for a few, someone nice like you. *(A rhyme based on an old TV public service announcement for venereal disease awareness.)*

However, true enlightenment doesn't make everything easier.

It awakens you to how "difficult" it all really is.

How weird is the larger world?

How difficult is truly living in such a world?

So weird, so difficult that it could drive one mad, and *has* driven many people mad.

Like Mr. Spock looking into the face of the ultimate alien being, really looking into the ultimate realities can dislodge one's entire mindset. That's one reason many people run from the challenge, or only go into it so far, or settle for simpler enlightenment substitutes such as drugs or adrenaline rushes.

THE MIScosity MANIFESTO

But you don't have to try to "get" it all.

You can simply admit that you can't, that nobody really can, and just take it as far as you feel comfortable with.

A century ago, the Dada artists of WWI and post-WWI Europe used imagery either whimsical or horrifying or both, to visualize a world that in their eyes had gone completely absurd.

In 1916, while what was known then as *"the* World War" still raged, German poet-author Hugo Ball (lower right) created *The Dada Manifesto*. It succinctly advocated Dada not as just another style of art-making but as an irreverent, playful approach toward life itself:

"Dada is the world soul, Dada is the pawnshop. Dada is the world's best lily-milk soap."

The Dadaists' partial successors, the Surrealists, took an even more explicitly political (or anti-political) stance. They spoke of the need to express Desire, modernity, and imagination: particularly the ability and will to imagine a better world, a world where Desire is unbound by mere politics or by overt oppression. A world where the needs of the heart and soul are sated, not just the needs for material goods.

Like a lot of modern art in the 20th century, the Surrealists were partly inspired by African "folk" art, and by ethnic struggles for not just autonomy but a larger sense of "freedom."

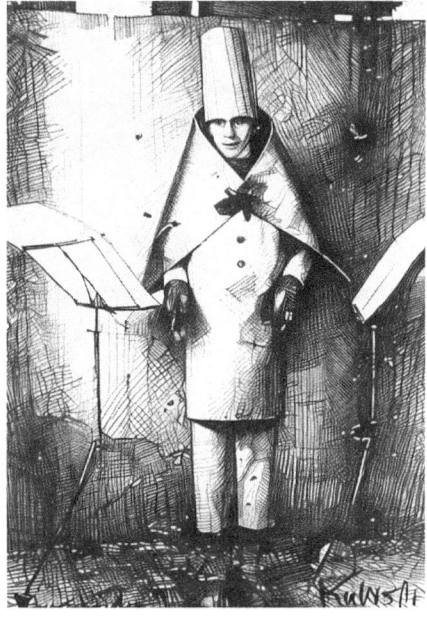

MY HEART DOES NOT BELONG TO DATA

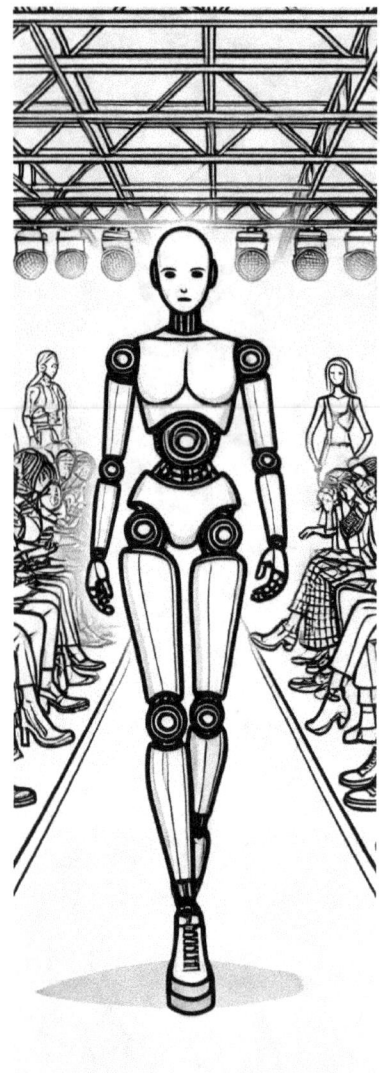

But, like anything, the notion of unbridled Desire can be corrupted, or taken into dangerous directions. It can devolve into mere drunken/drugged licentiousness, and from there into "rape culture."

No, I can't just "do any God damn thing I want" *(as per a Jim "Foetus" Thirlwell song)*. Not if that thing hurts people, harms the local/global environment, or violates the laws of simple interpersonal decency.

At the opposite of Dada (imaginative, whimsical) lies Data (precise, rigidly serious).

Data, along with (and in service to) Capital, is one of the dominant forces ruling our modern world.

Data's algorithms dictate factory production; its robots often carry out those dictates.

Data enabled the big health insurance companies to only insure healthy people.

Data enabled the big banks to create "mortgage-burger" securities, leading to the 2000s real estate "bubble" and its subsequent "pop."

Data enables big companies to squeeze out smaller competitors by finding and squeezing out every cent of expense, and by locating future sources of revenue. (One example: the e-commerce giant that, according to several lawsuits, hosted online "stores" from other companies, kept the data about what items in those "stores" sold best, then put up its own knockoff versions it sold directly.)

The juxtaposition of Dada and Data seems like a complete dichotomy—or is it a continuum, or a mirror?

Big Data can depict, parse, and juggle everything in all worlds real and fanciful—as long as it can be quantified, turned into complicated patterns of 1s and 0s.

Of course, some phenomena are more easily quantifiable than others. (Love, compassion, empathy, fear, etc. are hard to express as on/off switches, even as a whole lot of programmed on/off switches.)

And some things that can be quantified often aren't fully "sampled." For decades, foresters carefully measured the life and growth of trees from strictly the standpoint of their "crop" value. Thus, the "tree farm" concept, in which natural forest lands were remade as plantations for the seeding, growing, and harvesting of trees for wood and paper. But they didn't measure all the other benefits of real forests, the diversity and interdependence of life forms in such places. (See Richard Powers' 2018 novel *The Overstory*.)

Big Dada, however, can measure what Big Data can't.

Like the creative arts as a whole, it can tell us things about ourselves and our world that mere numbers (even really big quantities of numbers) will never really understand.

By manipulating, juxtaposing, subverting, and transcending visual "realism," Dada/Surrealism can show what's really out there, what really matters. Like the title of a history of gay "camp" culture, it's a "lie that tells the truth."

And, unlike data, Dada can freely admit to the limitations of individual awareness as well as the limitations of "knowledge."

An ordered tree farm; the seemingly 'chaotic' natural order of a real forest.

ACCEPTING THE ABSURD

The *Tao te Ching* discusses knowing by not knowing; as opposed to trying to know by narrowing and simplifying what there is to be known, to condense the world to something that can fit within our minds.

By admitting you don't know it all and never can, you're freed to look inward and outward at once, to sense the big-big-big picture.

And that's a lot healthier, for yourself and for the human race, than insisting that you (or your guru, preacher, or great leader) has all the answers.

"I fear the man of a single book."

That's attributed to St. Thomas Aquinas among others; but it's usually misinterpreted these days.

However, I tend to go along with the misinterpretation.

Aquinas apparently meant one should fear (respect) someone who's become a total expert in one precise field of learning; particularly if you're going to debate that person on the subject of that person's expertise.

But I say one should fear (be wary of) someone who knows a lot about just one thing, who has a too-narrow view of the world, who knows something in "depth" but not "breadth."

And you should really be wary of someone who uses a single book, or a single zeitgeist, as a one-size-fits-all guide to how everyone everywhere must live.

In that sense, it doesn't matter whether that one book is *Atlas Shrugged, Fear and Loathing in Las Vegas, Das Kapital, The Art of War, Dianetics, A Course in Miracles*, the aforementioned *Tao te Ching, The Tao of Pooh*, the King James Bible, or (especially) this one.

Any singular notion of how everything ought to be run will be at best very limiting and short-sighted; at worst deadly dangerous.

And besides (as per Hal Hartley's film *Surviving Desire*), "Knowing is not enough."

And you really never can know It All anyway.

Any human who claims to is, again, mistaken or dangerous or both.

•

I used to laugh at the bumper sticker slogan: *"Don't follow me. I'm lost too."*

Then I realized it's good to be lost. It's the only way to get anyplace new or different.

As I've briefly hinted, I am on the autism spectrum (in my case, not diagnosed until I was over 40). I know what it's like to want to Know. To finally have the key to "life, the universe, and everything."

But nobody can ever Know It All.

To even try is a task that inevitably leads to madness, and then you don't even know much of what you knew to begin with.

Better to live with the ignorance, to lovingly flow with the absurdity of It All.

We already mentioned Dada and Surrealism, which use the irrational to teach emotional truths.

(We'll be bouncing back and forth between topics all through the book. Life isn't linear, remember.)

FUN, SCARY, BOTH?

Lewis Carroll's Alice in Wonderland; Antonin Artaud; The Goon Show; Albert Camus.

There are many other forms of irrationality and absurdity in all its forms. We can learn from each of those forms.

More about these later. For now, here are a few:

- Zen koans; western aphorisms; puns and wordplay.
- Aristophanes, Plato, Aristotle.
- The "Theater of the Absurd," Antonin Artaud.
- Lewis Carroll. Edward Lear. Franz Kafka.
- The Futurists (too bad so many of them turned out to be Fascists).
- *The Goon Show* (a BBC Radio sketch comedy with a young Peter Sellers) and Monty Python.
- Thomas Hobbes' "Table of Absurdity."
- Film: Buñuel, Greenaway, Yoko Ono.
- The philosophy of Absurdism: Kierkegaard, Camus, the reaction to the destruction of Europe in WWII, "the fundamental disharmony between the individual's search for meaning and the meaninglessness of the universe." In other words, between the desire for Order and the reality of Chaos.

(*Francis Bacon*): "For if absurdity be the subject of laughter, doubt you but great boldness is seldom without some absurdity."

("What Is Absurdism," The Spiritual Life): "Acceptance of the Absurd: a solution in which one accepts the Absurd and continues to live in spite of it. Camus endorsed this solution, believing that by accepting the Absurd, one can achieve the greatest extent of one's freedom, and that by recognizing no religious or other moral constraints and by revolting against the Absurd while simultaneously accepting it as unstoppable, one could possibly be content from the personal meaning constructed in the process."

THE MISCosity MANIFESTO

Things absurdity is NOT:

- Smug irony. *(More on this later.)*
- Lame parody. *(More on this later also.)*
- Self-comforting cynicism, the kind that lets you conveniently give up on even trying.
- Bigotry that pretends to be merely a "satire" of bigotry.

•

Absurdity can often be fun.

Chaos, however, can often be scary.

Absurdity implies an order that is being subverted.

Chaos implies a lack of order, a lack of even plausible, workable Knowing.

If Chaos were absolute, there would be no stars, no habitable earth, no complex organisms (including you).

But if Order were absolute, there would be no novelty, no imagination, no true humanity.

(Cf. The *X Files* episode in which Mulder asks a real genie for world peace, and ends up (temporarily) with an uninhabited world. The lesson: where there are humans there will be conflict, and thus chaos.)

Thus, the notion of Order vs. Chaos in eternal oscillation and contention.

Artists Luigi Russolo and Ugo Piatti with instruments for futuristic music called 'Bruitism,' partly electrically operated, built by Russolo in 1913.

THE FUTILE WISH FOR ORDER

Let me explain what my own definition of chaos *isn't* (or maybe is, a little), by seeing how it's defined by others (we'll talk about a few of these later on):

- The pop-theory notion of loops, links, and an early concept of "chaos theory" (before that term was in wide use) in Douglas R. Hofstadter's 1979 book *Gödel, Escher, Bach*.
- Discordianism: either a parody religion, an attempt to create an order of the disorder, or a nerd/geek game as relevant as playing Dungeons & Dragons (except for its co-founder's strange connection to Lee Harvey Oswald).
- The vision of chaos as some kind of post-hippie Ragnarok promoted in the *Illuminatus!* novels by Robert Anton Wilson and Robert Shea.
- The vision propagated by UK alt-spiritual guru Aleister Crowley.
- The interface of hard science (even rocket science) and black magick pursued by John Whiteside Parsons, as depicted in the book and streaming series *Strange Angel*.
- Chaos magic(k), such as that by Genesis P-Orridge, a UK "difficult listening" musician and latter-day Crowley follower.
- Certain modern-day political anarchists, such as those of the "Black Bloc" variety, who seem to believe smashing bank branch windows creates a mortal blow to capitalist Order.
- The tech bros' worship of "disruption" and the motto "move fast; break things".
- The "alt-right" lust for destruction, especially for destroying the "social safety net."

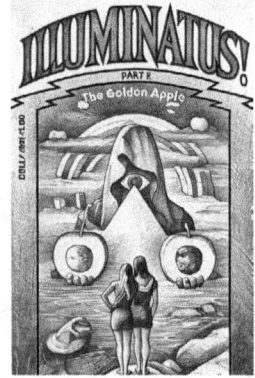

Strange Angel; *Aleister Crowley; The* Illuminatus! *Trilogy.*

THE MISCosity MANIFESTO

 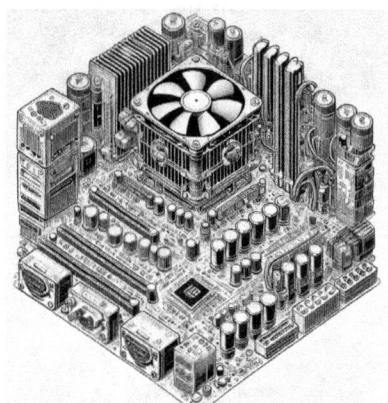

Two examples of complex visual harmony, inspired respectively by Tibetan Thangka mandala art and by computer circuitry.

One way the futile wish for Order appears is by positing theories and concepts about the ultimate Order, whether you can see it with your own senses or not.

This mindset can manifest itself as something as big as a "clockwork universe" theory, or as small as a conspiracy theory of one or another "Other" controlling human activities in secret cabals.

What if there is no grand conspiracy, no unified field theory, no through line?

That won't stop people from trying to find one.

We've discussed some of these attempts, including the "music of the spheres" and the "clockwork universe." Some others:

- The notion that we're all a computer simulation (a la *The Hitchhiker's Guide to the Galaxy* or *The Matrix*).
- The Hindus' massively complex pantheons; the Greeks' and Romans' relatively more compact ones.
- The notion that there is a great Director who assigns each of us with a "role" to play, and that we become sinners when we reject, or neglect to learn, that role.
- The notion among some Christians that this world is just a testing lab of sorts, with the purpose of determining which immortal souls get to go where.

DIFFERENT KINDS OF 'META' 24

Common to many of these theories is the notion of the oscillation of opposites, the great Binary.

The notion of the Binary is instilled into us, and has been since long before electronic computers' complex collections of 1s and 0s. Us/them, yin/yang, order/chaos, friend/foe, female/male, black/white or "minority"/white, rich/poor, free/slave, win/lose, wet/dry, light/dark, Left/Right, capitalist/communist, funny/serious.

But reducing everything to one or more binaries is itself an oversimplification, albeit a sometimes useful or at least convenient one.

Non-binary thinking challenges everything.

There is more than one way. But there are also more than two.

(As a supposed indigenous tribal arithmetic goes: "One, two, three, many.")

Part of living with the chaos (or at least the seeming chaos) is living with the complexities and diversities within everything.

In recent years, a few people have proposed a philosophic/aesthetic view that celebrates oscillation as "the natural order of the world." They call their belief system Metamodernism. As two of its early proponents, cultural theorists Timotheus Vermeulen and Robin van den Akker, wrote:

"Metamodernism moves for the sake of moving, attempts in spite of its inevitable failure; it seeks forever for a truth that it never expects to find... It oscillates between a modern enthusiasm and a postmodern irony, between hope and melancholy, between naïveté and knowingness, empathy and apathy, unity and plurality, totality and fragmentation, purity and ambiguity."

Luke Turner's 2011 *Metamodernist Manifesto* seeks to end *"...the inertia resulting from a century of modernist ideological naivety and the cynical insincerity of its antonymous bastard child [postmodernism]."*

Instead, Turner wants to explore *"the mercurial condition between and beyond irony and sincerity, naivety and knowingness, relativism and truth, optimism and doubt, in pursuit of a plurality of disparate and elusive horizons."* He calls this *"a pragmatic romanticism unhindered by ideological anchorage."*

In a 2015 article, Turner added that metamodernism doesn't *"propose any kind of utopian vision, although it does describe the climate in which a yearning for utopias, despite their futile nature, has come to the fore."*

Greg Dember's 2024 *Say Hello to Metamodernism* cites many examples from recent film, TV, and music to help understand *"today's culture of 'ironesty,' felt experience, and empathic reflexivity."*

To describe 'the structure of feeling' of metamodernism, Timotheus Vermeulen and Robin van den Akker 'used the metaphor of a pendulum continually oscillating from the sincere seriousness of modernism to the ironic playfulness of postmodernism.' (Wikipedia)

Simone Weil.

In one definition of *metamodernism*, "meta" stands for Plato's concept of *metaxy* or *metaxu*, which denotes the middle ground between two poles of existence (Heaven and Earth, God and Man, Infinite and Finite, Physical and Spiritual, etc.).

As Simone Weil interpreted it:

"No human being should be deprived of his metaxu, that is to say of those relative and mixed blessings (home, country, traditions, culture, etc.) which warm and nourish the soul and without which, short of sainthood, a human life is not possible.

"The true earthly blessings are metaxu. We can respect those of others only in so far as we regard those we ourselves possess as metaxu. This implies that we are already making our way towards the point where it is possible to do without them. For example, if we are to respect foreign countries, we must make of our own country, not an idol, but a stepping-stone towards God....

"The essence of created things is to be intermediaries. They are intermediaries leading from one to the other, and there is no end to this."

One of the most effective, yet deceptively simple, ways to disrupt ordered logic is the *paradox*.

That's *"a logically self-contradictory statement or a statement that runs contrary to one's expectation."* (Eric W. Weisstein quoted at Wikipedia)

In writing, it's *"commonly used to engage a reader to discover an underlying logic in a seemingly self-contradictory statement or phrase."* (literarydevices.net)

"The ancient Greeks were well aware that a paradox can take us outside our usual way of thinking. They combined the prefix para- ('beyond' or 'outside of') with the verb dokein ('to think'), forming paradoxos, an adjective meaning 'contrary to expectation.'" (Merriam-Webster.com)

A paradox can take the form of a joke, a Zen *koan* (such as the ol' "sound of one hand clapping" bit), a math problem, or a philosophical dilemma. Or all of the above.

Many famous philosophical paradoxes trace their origins to Greek philosopher Zeno of Elea, who intended them to illustrate his "monistic" belief *"that only one single entity exists that makes up all of reality."*

Among "Zeno's paradoxes":

- The person who says he always lies, even when he says he's currently lying (as Captain Kirk used against an android in the original *Star Trek* episode "I, Mudd").
- A linear movement divided into ever-smaller halves, never resulting in the person or thing reaching their destination (like the "half the distance to the goal" penalty in American football).

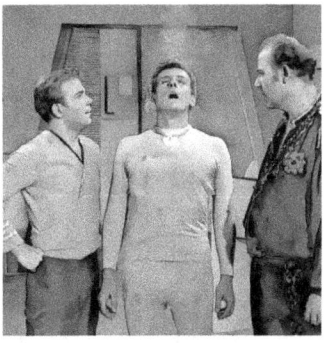

SHIVA THE PHYSICIST?

One of the most famous paradoxes of all time is Rene Magritte's 1929 painting *The Treachery of Images*, featuring a hyper-realistic image of a pipe above the words: *"This is not a pipe."*

The simple answer to the contradiction: Yes, it's just a *picture* of a pipe.

But one can also use the contradiction as a mental springboard, to ponder questions of reality and illusion, among others.

Philosopher-historian Michel Foucault (billed by the *NY Review of Books* as "France's great wizard of paradox") wrote a book-length homage to Magritte's work. *"By exploring the nuances and ambiguities of Magritte's visual critique of language, he finds the painter less removed than previously thought from the pioneers of modern abstraction." (Publisher's blurb)*

You don't have to delve as deeply into a paradox as Foucault does to realize how the exercise can help you to maintain contradictory ideas, letting them oscillate and pulsate in your brain.

(F. Scott Fitzgerald, 1936): "The test of a first-rate intelligence is the ability to hold two opposed ideas in the mind at the same time, and still retain the ability to function. One should, for example, be able to see that things are hopeless and yet be determined to make them otherwise."

THE MISCosity MANIFESTO

Hinduism's main deities have many names and forms in different sects.

One of the most important of these deities is Lord Shiva (also known as Mahadeva, Neelakantha, Rudra, Shambhu, Tatajara, and many more).

Shiva Tatajara is known for symbolizing the endless dance of creation and destruction. According to the Agamas (a group of Hindu sacred scriptures), this dance has five stages: *"the birth of the world, its maintenance, its destruction, the soul's obscuration, and liberation."*

According to Fritjof Capra's *The Tao of Physics* (1975), there are many *"parallels between modern physics and Eastern mysticism."*

One of these compares Shiva's dance to quantum field theory, which features what Capra calls the "energy dance" of subatomic particles, *"a pulsating process of creation and destruction... the basis of all existence and of all natural phenomena."*

Nothing is eternal. Nothing is fixed. Everything is always in motion.

ASSEMBLING THE SELF

De Beauvoir; Sartre; a 'self' assembled from parts.

The existentialist thinker/author Jean-Paul Sartre wrote of how "existence precedes essence" and "the non-existence, or non-importance, of the self." As comedian Stephen Fry interprets Sartre, "there is no design for a human being."

Sartre thought that false illusions of certainty and necessity obscure both what we're really made of and what we really need to do. What we become in life is up to us.

Yet this uncertainty (and, yes, this absurdity) makes creating your own path through life so important. When we do this, we're not only creating ourselves, but deciding what a human being should be.

Sartre's colleague/partner Simone de Beauvoir, in her 1947 book *The Ethics of Ambiguity*, depicts each human as both a first-person "subject" and a third-person "object" or "thing"; as encompassing both "freedom" and "facticity" (a type of order, a set entity). Each of us has freedom of choice, but it's constrained by the physical, social, political, and other limits of one's body and social standing. De Beauvoir defines "ethics" as *"the triumph of freedom over facticity."* We must continually re-create ourselves, and also re-connect with others. As a result:

'...we are absolutely free today if we choose to will our existence in its finiteness, a finiteness which is open on the infinite.'

Gary Cox's book *How to Be an Existentialist* insists existentialism is not a philosophy of despair or resignation but one of self-will. Your being, your emotions, your mindset, are not "baked in" from birth. They're influenced by your background, your life history so far. But you have the power to remake them, to be the active maker of your life. You can, as Cox puts it, *"get real, get a grip, and stop making excuses."*

My own vision of Chaos is closer to that of the Greeks and the Hebrews, as "the primordial state of being."

And the old yin/yang again, as the necessary counterpart to Order.

I'm not promoting it. I'm saying it's out there; it always was, and always will be, out there.

And this "out there" includes that which is within each of us.

Instead of the term "Chaos," with its negative connotations, you could instead think of it as:

The General Eclectic Company.

The Big Everything, in all its massive, multivalent glory.

A big, wide, wonderful, scary, confusing, frustrating, confusing, joyous universe.

A world where everything is falling apart, dispersing, dividing, dissolving ("entropy," in more than just the physical realm).

But also, a world where everything is combining, recombining, multiplying, growing, building.

Self-help lecturer Tara Brach preaches a Buddhist-inspired "radical acceptance" of the Chaos.

This does NOT mean simply going with the flow, or allowing people (including yourself) to continue doing evil things, ignoring cruelty and injustice in the world.

It means to *"embrace ourselves with all our pain, fear and anxieties, and to step lightly yet firmly on the path of understanding and compassion."* (From the cover blurb by Thich Nhat Hanh for Brach's book Radical Acceptance.)

The Greek god Chaos; a Hebrew hamsa *symbol (to ward off evil); an American icon of power and conglomeration.*

THE COMPLEX AND THE COMPLICATED 32

Alan Watts' 1951 book *The Wisdom of Insecurity* attested that the only way we can learn anything truly worth knowing is by accepting all that we don't know, and can never know:

"To discover the ultimate Reality of life—the Absolute, the eternal, God—you must cease to try to grasp it in the forms of idols. These idols are not just crude images, such as the mental picture of God as an old gentleman on a golden throne. They are our beliefs, our cherished preconceptions of the truth, which block the unreserved opening of the mind and heart to reality. The legitimate use of images is to express the truth, not to possess it."

Respecting, even loving, the chaos doesn't mean you need to artificially create more of it for yourself.

Overstimulation is another false definition of the Chaos—whether that's accomplished via drugs, or by any of the various psychological addictions (gambling, dangerous sex, unhealthy relationships, video games, outrage-talk radio, social media, etc.).

My definition of the Chaos is not about being manic, or confused, or addled.

It's not about succumbing to emotional distress, or fear, or frustration.

It's not about entering into (by choice, instinct, or learned habit) a chaotic personal mental/emotional state.

It's about accepting the massiveness of it all, in the outside world and in yourself; accepting one's status as an integral part of all this.

You could start on a relatively simple level by pondering:

- *Pi*, the chaotic number at the heart of all geometry and therefore all existence. Never resolving; never repeating.
- Fractals, the golden spiral and the golden ratio, sacred geometry, and how repeating patterns appear in things and people alike.
- The Complex and the Complicated, and the differences between them.

    (One definition: A "complicated" novel or film simply has lots of things going on. A "complex" story can explore the interplay of big and little emotional effects within even the simplest of plots.)

Explore these seriously, and you may find an "empirical" way of thinking that can apply not just in the sciences but in all of life.

REVOLUTIONARY VS. EVOLUTIONARY 34

There are infinite connections of plant and animal life.

That's one of the lessons of the Neukom Vivarium, the "nurse log" exhibit at the Olympic Sculpture Park in my home city, Seattle.

At the exhibit's center is a piece of plant life in a state of long-term decay. It's become the home, the host, and the food for a lot of bugs, rodents, flowers, and other beings.

The Vivarium is a "microcosm." In the "macrocosm" of the "real" world, trees and fungi often have shared root systems. They're biological "networks" whose above-the-ground parts are multiple "nodes."

James Lovelock and Lynn Margulis's "Gaia Hypothesis" (named for the Greek goddess that embodies the earth) asserts that the whole planet—including all its organisms—is one big interdependent system, all synergistic and self-regulating. Some scientists think this theory goes a little too far. But even if you don't believe the world's one all-encompassing entity, the world's component entities (organic and otherwise) affect one another in endless big and small ways.

It's also the lesson of Rachel Carson's groundbreaking book *Silent Spring*. In it, Carson tracks how a chemical (DDT) intended to kill human-unfriendly bugs (mosquitoes, fire ants) ended up killing or sickening vast swaths of birds and other critters, while infiltrating the human food supply.

And it's the lesson of how the medications (diuretics, antidepressants, etc.) people take end up in their sewage, make it past "treatment," get into the open seas, and then get into the fish and the whole aquatic food chain.

The human body has been studied for millennia, and we're still learning stuff about it. How the respiratory system's connected to the circulatory system, the digestive system's connected to.... *"The music goes round and round and it comes out here."* (from a 1930s song)

The brain itself is still a vastly more complex structure and process than any human-made computer.

You are a finely tuned system of blood, bones, organs, skin, marrow, muscles, sinews, synapses, axons, neurons, fats, acids, and assorted fluids. And those are composed of cells—about 100 trillion cells in all. Thankfully, most of them don't need your conscious attention, at least not most of the time.

•

There's a theory called the "Many Worlds Interpretation."

Based on quantum mechanics, the theory asserts that there are many (perhaps infinite) universes, and that everything that could have happened in our own past did happen in one of the alternate universes.

Even if you accept the possibility, those sci-fi "alternate universe" plots still almost always get it wrong.

There could probably never be a pair of worlds in which the same characters with the same names, only "evil" instead of "good," would have the same ranks on the crews of spaceships with the same names and designs.

Any one change of fate anywhere could have sent the course of our history in wild other directions. Different people would have been born, done different things, had different children, etc.

NON-LINEARITY BEFORE THE INTERNET 36

In Europe, the printing press led to massive social upheavals. In Asia, not so much.

By the law of averages, the main invented things of human society would still have eventually been invented in these alternate Earths (along with the alloys and other materials needed to make them, the machines to build and transport them, et al.).

But they would all have come with different sets of "cultural baggage."

Different cultures react differently to different new things (machines, metals, industries, farming practices, human visitors).

James Burke, in his BBC documentary series *Connections*, noted how the kinds of inventions that "revolutionized" European society simply "blended into" the more "stable" (or stodgy) East Asian societies. Imperial China and Japan were able to absorb the arrival of gunpowder, movable-type printing, et al. while keeping the royal families and the feudal and caste systems mostly untouched. While in Europe, something as simple as new formulas for clothing dyes (invented, but not commercially exploited, in England) led to Germany's rise as a global player in chemicals and drugs of all sorts.

That's like a Western History version of those "Choose Your Own Adventure" books, or early computer adventure games like *Zork* and *Myst*.

The concepts behind those books and games are, at heart, more than mere games. They're also a structural tool, one also used in non-"gaming" contexts.

THE MISCosity MANIFESTO

Several highbrow literary authors have played with multi-linear or non-linear sequences.

Julio Cortazar's 1963 novel *Hopscotch* tells a story you can read from the first chapter to the last, or in an alternate order as mentioned in the author's opening "Table of Instructions."

Jorge Luis Borges' (an Argentinian, like Cortazar) 1941 story *The Garden of Forking Paths* envisions a vast, intricate novel (Borges didn't write novels; he wrote short stories *about* novels) that would also be also a vast, intricate labyrinth, one "in which all men would lose their way."

The Situationists, a post-Surrealist group of French writers and philosophers, went on semi-organized strolls ("*derives*") through the streets of Paris. They took random paths and turns, willing to discover (and pontificate upon) whatever they saw.

And your traditional print newspaper is a package of long and short texts, and images that sometimes illustrate the text pieces and sometimes don't; plus the self-contained messages of advertisers. They can be read, skimmed, or ignored in any order.

THE MAP IS NOT THE TERRITORY—OR IS IT?

In 1945, engineer Vannevar Bush wrote a magazine article, "As We May Think." It proposed a machine he called the "Memex," which would store vast amounts of information on reels of microfilm. Users could follow cross references between documents via "coded symbols."

In his self-published 1974 book *Computer Lib/Dream Machines*, early computer scientist Ted Nelson (son of actress Celeste Holm) promoted the concept of "hypertext" (a term Nelson coined in 1963), in which individual documents would contain embedded "links" to other documents on related subjects. Nelson's proposed implementation of this concept, Project Xanadu, was (and possibly still is) too complicated to build (on both the software and "content" levels).

(*Computer Lib* also included the slogan "Everything is Deeply Intertwingled," which this book intends to confirm.)

In 1987, Apple released Bill Atkinson's application HyperCard. It simplified the hypertext concept into something that could run on early Macs, and was a major hit.

A few years after that, Tim Berners-Lee and a small crew came up with the World Wide Web, a hypertext system in which documents could be linked to other documents, even if they'd been posted by other entities to other computers on the same network connection.

That simple scripting trick birthed the great digital primordial soup.

You all know the virtual life forms that evolved from those first plain-text amoebae: Cute cat pictures. "Memes." Trolling, doxxing, death threats, and conspiracy theories. Dead or dying newspapers and record labels. "Swiping right." Forums for lonely LGBT teens stuck in small towns. Porn fetishes you might never have imagined could exist. Podcasters, bloggers, vloggers, and "influencers." Doomscrolling (as symbolized below).

But also: A profoundly different way of thinking about things. Endless "linkage" rather than linearity. Eternal digressions. People are learning, all over again, the value of Breadth as well as Depth.

J.A. Ginsburg has worked as a science journalist, art curator, website producer, and book packager, among many other things. (She calls herself a "silo-skipper," jumping between "silos of expertise" across industries and subjects.) She says silo-skippers *"are adept at analogy, talk in tangents and delight in digression. They savor stray facts, knowing that sooner or later one just might fill in a critical blank and, like a long-lost puzzle piece, complete a picture. They constantly scan for connections across disciplines and sectors. For them, understanding the lack of connection can be just as intriguing as finding a match."*

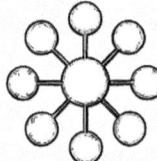

You've probably heard of *Six Degrees of Separation*, John Guare's play-turned-film built around the notion that each of us is six connections away from anyone else. (Or its spoof project, "Six Degrees of Kevin Bacon." My own "Bacon number": 3.)

The idea has a long history with its own sequence of connections, as detailed in Albert-Laszlo Barabási's book *Linked*. Barabási says the concept may have begun with *Chains*, a 1929 short story by Hungarian writer Frigyes Karinthy.

Then in 1967, Harvard prof Stanley Milgram conducted a research study on the topic. His study cited 5.5 as a "median number" of "intermediate persons," not an absolute limit, between any two people. And that only applied to links between people living in the US, not the whole world.

Barabási's book also said any World Wide Web document was "on average only 19 clicks away from any other." (However, that was almost two decades ago; the Web's size and complexity have gotten enormously bigger since then.)

Jorge Luis Borges' 1946 story *On Rigor in Science* imagines a country devoted to the science of map-making. The country's best minds decide that the most accurate map would have to be the same size as the area it represented (foreshadowing the film *Synecdoche New York*, in which a filmmaker creates a full-size replica of Manhattan inside a giant warehouse).

To fully depict the full spectrum of humanity would also require a "map" big enough to include everyone living— and everyone who ever had lived.

And maybe not even a flat map. Perhaps something more like a hollow sphere, with everyone as pinpoints in relation to everyone else.

THE MISCosity MANIFESTO

Brief examples of how our lives and fates are interdependent, which might include:

- A linear sequence of encounters, from person A to person B, then B to C, etc., as in the play and film *La Ronde*.
- A kids' "game of telephone."
- A Richard Scarry-like town square setting, in which friends, relatives, and total strangers interact in some of the countless other ways.
- Worked-up crowds at a gospel church (with a choir), a soccer match (with teamwork on display), a concert (with a band in sync), etc.

But these days, a lot of people report feeling alone, even in a crowd. To contrast, some works that illustrate the lack of needed connections:

- A *Where's Waldo*-like detail of individuals in a mall or a park by themselves, centered on one particularly forlorn person.
- The title concept in Robert Putnam's book *Bowling Alone*.
- The R.E.M. traffic jam video ("Everybody Hurts") with people literally isolated by their vehicles.
- A family dinner where nobody looks at anyone else.
- A group of teenagers, each staring into her own smartphone.

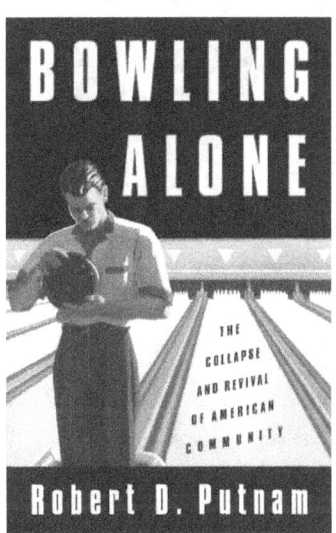

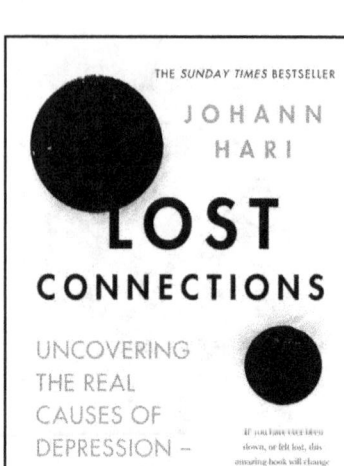

Johann Hari's book *Lost Connections* claims loneliness (as well as a lack of a purpose in life, past abuse, and other psychological issues) among the real causes of so much depression and anxiety in the developed world.

We need connection as much as we need to eat, drink, sleep, and breathe.

Another cause Hari cites for a global pandemic of depression and anxiety is alienation, a feeling of not belonging in one's surroundings.

But what if that's just a natural reaction to modern existence?

Betty Friedan and others noted that the post-WWII, socially prescribed role of the perfect homemaker, helped by modern labor-saving household products, was stifling and smothering to many who'd tried to live up to it. Externally, these affluent women "had it made." Internally, not so.

Similarly, Hari says, many people of many genders may seem to "have it all," at least materialistically; but they can feel hollow, trapped in meaningless soul-crushing work to attain material goods they don't really need, with no true friends or companions.

(*From* The Xenofeminist Manifesto: A Politics for Alienation, *authored under the collective byline "Laboria Cuboniks"*): "We are all alienated—but have we ever been otherwise?")

(*Attributed to Jiddu Krishnamurti*): "It is no measure of health to be well-adjusted to a profoundly sick society."

THE MISCosity MANIFESTO

So:

- You are not a mindless, soulless cog in a big "machine."
- And you are not a self-enclosed, self-sustaining, solo entity.
- You are not data.
- You are not an algorithm.
- You are not a demographic or a psycho-graphic.
- You are not your credit score.
- You are not your job or your possessions or your street address.
- You are not a target market.
- You are not (only) your nationality, ethnicity, skin color, gender, sexual preference, etc.
- You are not (only) some other person's wife/husband, girlfriend/boyfriend, child, parent, sibling, boss, employee, acolyte, soldier, customer, servant, model, or muse.
- You are not a label, even if you're the one doing the labeling.
- You may not even really be the gender you were born into.

(Zat Rana, "Why You Are Not Who You Say You Are," 2018): "You are not the words you define yourself by, and I am not the person with a disposition that can be captured by a written scene."

Who and what you really are:
- "A child of the universe."
- A node of the whole networked consciousness of the human species (and maybe of "Gaia," and maybe of a universe-wide consciousness).
- A being of spirit, mind, and body (*a la* the YMCA triangle).
- Someone with "agency" (also known as "free will"), and with an ability to always keep learning and growing.
- A product of your genes, your upbringing, your heritage, and untold influences and experiences, big and small, past and present.
- A product of your thinking about all these things, including yourself.
- A part of families, biological and "virtual."

And you are someone who is created by, and who helps to create and re-create, the culture around you, in your circles of friends/co-workers-acquaintances, your neighborhood, your social media worlds, your town, your nation, and your and our planet.

Don't ever forget that people's everyday interactions create a culture. Not a culture dictated from some far-off church, government, high-art establishment, or media industry, but culture as lived "in real life" by real people.

You have every right to ignore the dictates of fashion, or of peers (in social media or in "real" life), or of media ("mainstream" or "alternative").

And you have every right (even a duty) to proclaim how you think societies should be run, even if it's not what authority figures (in your town, school, or nation) want to hear.

Thomas Jefferson and Martin Luther King, among others, have talked about the moral imperative to rebel against an unjust government and/or society.

To demand a better world, and to help create such a world.

At the time this is being written, society and government are under tremendous pressure, in my nation and several others.

Well-funded, multi-tentacled forces actively promote a worldview built on deliberate ignorance, blind outrage, unquestioned obedience, racist/sexist bigotry, rapacious greed, and ego-driven brutality.

Some of their adherents claim to advocate "free speech" and even "freedom," even as they try to try to turn this country into a dictatorship in all but name.

But also, millions have come together in hundreds of large and small "intersectional" groups to stop this descent into darkness, to demand accountability and democracy, to protect the planet, and to increase rights and respect for a wider swath of the populace.

(Ursula K. Le Guin): "There are great powers, outside the government and in it, trying to legislate the return of darkness. We are not great powers. But we are the light. Nobody can put us out. May all of you shine very bright and steady, today and always."

WHO'S A 'REAL' AMERICAN?

And the nation's also changing in other, more permanent, ways.

Many cities and counties are now "majority minority." Before too long, Americans of European descent will be less than half the national population.

Many suburbs and exurbs are now more ethnically diverse than the gentrifying cities they surround.

Same-sex marriage has become the law of the land.

Gay, lesbian, transgender, non-binary, and genderqueer people are asserting their right to exist and to be respected.

With some major exceptions (the tech industries, corporate boardrooms, Republican politicians), professions across the workforce are becoming, at least gradually, less male and less white.

The same social media platforms that have helped to empower hate groups have also helped to empower victims of child sexual abuse, small-town gay teens, escapees from cults, people on the autism spectrum, etc.

Canadians used to say that, unlike the US's stated ideal of a monocultural "melting pot," Canada tried instead to become a "mosaic" of different cultures.

Now both countries are becoming more mosaic-y (more truly "miscellaneous") than ever.

There's an idea, held by many people over the centuries, that the "real" America (or the "real" Canada, the "real" England, etc.) lies outside of the main cities, in the rural heartland where the pace is slow and the people are more "traditional" (i.e., conservative, monocultural, and ethnically "pure").

I don't buy it.

The "real" America is, and always has been, the whole of America.

City and town farm and suburb.

White and Black and Brown and Red and more.

Straight and gay and bi and trans and more.

Protestant and Catholic and Jewish and Hindu and Muslim and more.

This country has always been diverse, even when it claimed not to be.

And now, at long bloody last, more of us recognize it.

Could we now truly, finally, be "more American" than we've ever been before?

But certain powerful corners of business, government, and media want to divide us—race against race, gender against gender, rich against poor, neighbor against neighbor.

Why? To divide and conquer, of course.

Marketers want you to believe their products are "for" your "tribe" (subculture, age group, gender, etc.).

Right-wing politicians are often marketed as the candidates "for" rural, working-class, and "low education" voters. Just as there were cigarettes marketed as "for" women. (With similar end results to the "clientele.")

NOBODY'S SUPERIOR

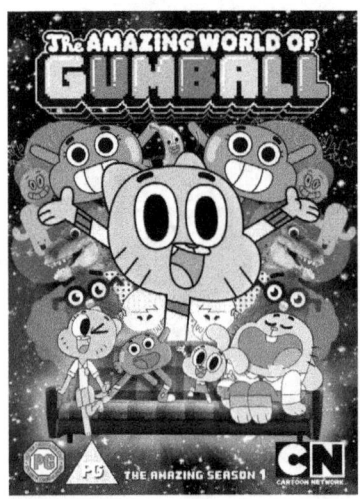

We're all bozos on this bus.

(That comes from an LP by the Firesign Theatre, whose farcical plays on vinyl records helped keep audio drama alive in the years between old-time radio and podcasts. The troupe's members were '60s generation adults who'd been kids during old time radio's heyday.)

Not only is the whole human race interconnected, it (like the universe itself) is more diverse than you imagine, than perhaps you even can imagine.

Everybody's 'weird.'
Everybody's 'different.'

A schoolteacher once supposedly asked her students if they considered their families to be "normal." None did.

(Grunkle Stan, on the Disney Channel series Gravity Falls: *"Everybody here's a tad strange. Except, of course, for Tad Strange.")*

(From Xav Clarke's theme to Cartoon Network's The Amazing World of Gumball): *"Nobody's a nobody and everybody is weird like you and me."*

And we've all got to learn to get along, as equals, not as masters and servants or as bosses and underlings or as leaders and followers. What we need to become (as a whole species) is something we've not really been (as a whole species) to date.

And nobody possesses any innate "superiority" over other people.

Certainly not any "superiority" based on such flimsy premises as circumstances of birth, ancestry, belief systems, or dietary regimens.

THE MISCosity MANIFESTO

- There is no master race.
- There is also no master gender,
- no master nationality,
- no master religion,
- no master economic system,
- and no master subculture.

Nobody is innately "inferior" either.

Dehumanizing 'The Other' isn't just something 'those people' do.

It's easy to dis other people for, well, dissing other people. It's harder to admit you've been tempted to do it also. (More about this in a bit.)

One of the key points of the whole MISCosity premise is:

- People who are different from you *are people too*.
- Yes, even *them*.

Depending on your own circumstances, your own Others could include:

- Women, men, Blacks, Hispanics, whites, gays, straights, transgenders, cisgenders, urbanites, suburbanites, ruralites, Muslims, Christians, "Other" kinds of Christians, feminists, feminists who don't agree with your own definition of feminism, meat eaters, vegans, jocks, stoners, intellectuals, TV viewers, southerners, northeasterners, Californians, immigrants, WASPs, the poor, the rich, and (yep) Jews.

CONFORMIST NON-CONFORMISTS

In 1959, MAD magazine noted that "more and more clods are trying to be different, so there are more and more Non-Conformists! And all these Non-Conformists are so busy Conforming to not being Conformists, they all wind up Conforming to their Non-Conformism!"

The response in the article (with uncredited text beside George Woodbridge's art): the "MAD Non-Conformist":

- Their favorite music: "...bird calls, tap dancing and exercise lessons, transcriptions of Senate committee hearings, Gallagher & Shean*, the Singing Lady*, and theme music from famous monster movies."
- Their favorite films: "...the Dempsey-Firpo fight, Sally Rand's Fan Dance, old Ben Turpin comedies, and Tom Mix pre-adult westerns."
- Their favorite clothes: "...glamorous opera capes, roomy knickers, comfortable Keds, and lightweight pith helmets which offer good protection in bad weather and provide storage space for day's lychee nuts."

While the article's pure satire, I'm proud to have known people whose tastes (in some areas) are remarkably similar to these. They love what they love, and don't have to prove themselves to anybody.

MAD, in its heyday, was itself an example of cross-cultural critique. Essentially, it reflected New York local culture (the world of delis, Jewish and Italian extended families, and street jargon) criticizing New York export culture (big business, mass media, advertising).

Gallagher and Shean were a vaudeville music-comedy act. The Singing Lady was a 1940s radio show, devoted less to singing than to telling children's stories.

All except for a small group of bravely idiotic MAD readers — to whom this article is dedicated — mainly because, in this article, we explain in nauseating detail...

HOW TO BE A MAD NON-CONFORMIST

PICTURES BY GEORGE WOODBRIDGE

THE MISCosity MANIFESTO

Some white folk claim, "I don't see color."

These folk believe it's a progressive stance.

Not really.

It denies other people's struggles, their heritage, their stories. People of other ethnicities, nationalities, genders, etc. have lives and identities of their own.

Don't just think of them only in relation to your own life story.

The old TV trope of the "good and evil twins" has a distant basis in reality. Even among people with the same family (and DNA) background, everyone has needs, desires, ambitions, likes, dislikes, loves, and a body, mind, soul, and history all their own.

In 2009, Nigerian writer Chimamanda Ngozi Adichie made a TED Talk about "The Danger of the Single Story." As David Brooks later summarized it, Adichie talked about how *"complex human beings and situations are reduced to a single narrative: when Africans, for example, are treated solely as pitiable poor, starving victims with flies on their faces."*

As Adichie said in her talk, *"The single story creates stereotypes, and the problem with stereotypes is not that they are untrue, but that they are incomplete. They make one story become the only story."*

African-Americans, as an example, don't merely exist to inspire white musicians, or for anti-racist whites to nobly support.

"Positive" but one-dimensional stereotypes (the simple but wise native, the black spiritual teacher to the white hero, the American Indian warrior) can be just as damaging as negative stereotypes.

CAN HATE BE CURED?

Gregor Mendel;
Gabor Maté;
Ijeoma Oluo.

Biologist Gregor Johann Mendel was one of the first to see the need for "biodiversity" between and within species.

I believe that also applies in our species—ethnically and culturally. Addiction expert Dr. Gabor Maté asserts that *"all addictions originate in trauma and emotional loss."*

Not all people who face such traumas turn to drugs or other addictive behaviors to escape the physical and/or emotional pain; not all of those people become addicted.

But Maté claims all addictions have trauma as one (in many cases the main) cause. To alleviate this: "Repairing that disconnect involves work. It can involve psychological work, emotional work, physical work, and spiritual work but the key to remember is that it is available at any time, and that is good news."

Johann Hari calls connection the only real cure for addiction.

If we are to treat the victims of drug/alcohol addictions with empathy and compassion (and my mom, the queen bee of AA in her town for more than 30 years, would say we should), we should treat these victims of non-chemical drug addictions likewise—to the extent we can.

Sally Kohn's book *The Opposite of Hate* described an online chat between activist writer Ijeoma Oluo (author of *So You Want to Talk About Race*) and several online racist trolls. One of these young men eventually apologized for how he'd treated her. Kohn described it as an example of compassion overcoming hate.

Oluo disagreed with Kohn's interpretation: *"That was a long painful day to get one teenager to just be like 'I'm sorry'... I would love to see the long-term systemic impact on structural racism that had compared to the impact it had on my well-being."*

THE MISCosity MANIFESTO

But still, Kohn has a point. Though it can be horrendously difficult, to the point of risking your own mental health (especially with total strangers who've openly proclaimed they hate you, as in Oluo's case), connecting can be the key to healing so many of our ills, on micro- and macro-levels.

•

Just as you're supposed to put on your own oxygen mask first in an aircraft emergency, so should you keep a watch on your own emotional and mental health as you try to help others find theirs. I define empathy and compassion as seeing the humanity in each human, not in spite of the "differences" but encompassing them, celebrating them.

Basking in the oscillations and opposites. Feeling what another person feels, or at least making a sincere try at it.

Caring. Giving a damn. Meaning it. Proving it in your actions, not just in your words.

The idea behind prosthetic "empathy bellies" for dads-to-be, and "immersive experiences" (sometimes using virtual-reality goggles) where people who aren't blind, deaf, or in wheelchairs are shown a sliver of what it's like to be those things, is to get you to feel someone else's existence in your own mind and body, at least for a specified period of time.

But empathy doesn't require fully inhabiting the mind and body of another.

But it does require at least an attempt at feeling how they feel, and at roughly estimating their mental constructs and history.

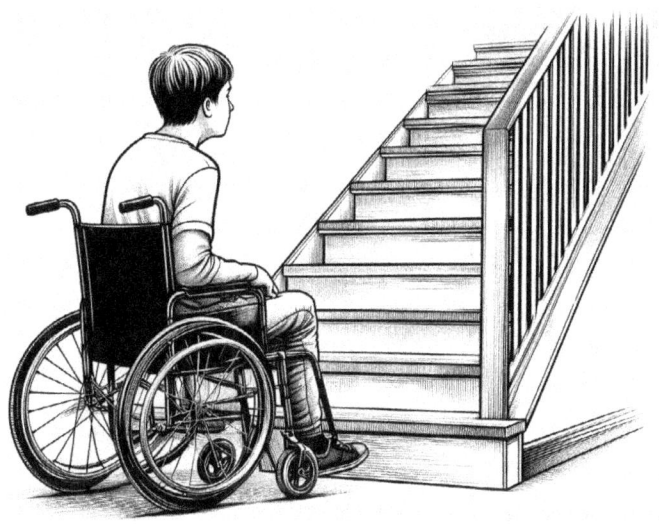

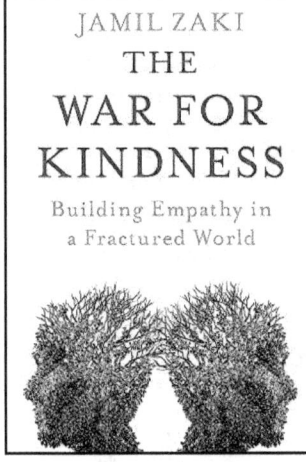

(Dear White America author Tim Wise): "Empathy—real empathy, not the situational and utterly phony kind that most any of us can muster when social convention calls for it—requires that one be able to place oneself in the shoes of another, and to consider the world as they must consider it. It requires that we be able to suspend our own culturally-ingrained disbelief long enough to explore the possibility that perhaps the world doesn't work as we would have it, but rather as others have long insisted it did."

(Jamil Zaki, The War for Kindness: Building Empathy in a Fractured World): "Most people understand empathy as more or less a feeling in itself—I feel your pain—but it's more complicated than that. 'Empathy' actually refers to several different ways we respond to each other. These include identifying what others feel (cognitive empathy), sharing their emotions (emotional empathy), and wishing to improve their experiences (empathetic concern)."

•

People used to believe that autistic people didn't have empathy. A socio-economic reform movement in France in the early 2000s, "Post-Autistic Economics," got its name from the assumption that people with autism, just like top-down economic theories and their adherents, lacked the ability to sense other people's feelings and suffering.

That notion was popularized in the 1980s by researchers Simon Baron-Cohen (filmmaker Sacha Baron-Cohen's cousin) and Uta Frith (art-rock guitarist Fred Frith's sister-in-law). They claimed autistic people lacked a "theory of mind," the ability to imagine other people's thoughts and feelings.

Later researchers and advocates, and autistic people themselves (who'd gotten tired of being talked about but not listened to), have denounced that premise, along with the one-size-fits-all definition of autism itself, in favor of a "spectrum" of conditions (also known as "neurodiversity"—even our minds are MISCous!).

Indeed, some autism-diagnosed people might be more, not less, sensitive to others. To these folks, a room full of other people talking can give off an emotional or psychic cacophony as well as an aural cacophony, enough to make the person want to withdraw into their own self.

(Autism advocate Liane Kupferberg Carter): "Some people on the spectrum may struggle with empathy; others can feel overwhelmed by other people's feelings. Then there is everyone in between. You know what? That's why we call it a spectrum."

Steve Silberman's book *NeuroTribes: The Legacy of Autism and the Future of Neurodiversity* asserts, according to its publisher's blurb, that "*neurological differences such as autism, dyslexia, and ADHD are not errors of nature or products of the toxic modern world, but the result of natural variations in the human genome.*"

To Silberman and Carter, "neurotypical" people may need to empathize with people "on the spectrum" just as much as vice versa.

"I've got TONS to say! You're just not listening!"

THE GOLDEN RULE 2.0

Practical love in everyday life is one of those things that's easy to talk about and a lot harder to do.

A few prescriptions for this (your mileage may vary, as may your situation):

As yourself:

- Be kind and forgiving to yourself.
- Be honest about your feelings.
- Don't say (or type) things just to make you feel powerful.
- Be thankful. Be grateful. Even if it's just for living one more day.
- Work at improving your own "moral compass."
- Remember: your opinions aren't facts, your preferences aren't virtues, you're not more important than anyone else.
- Seek the truth; don't insist you already have it.
- In traffic, don't treat the other drivers as the enemy but as compatriots, all striving to get somewhere.
- Volunteer at a place where you'll do humble, basic tasks (cleaning, child care, yard work).
- Take an art class, in a discipline you're not already good at.
- Let go of the "zero-sum" mentality ("for someone else to win, I must lose").
- Try to let go of all unnecessary binary thinking.
- Live as if the rules apply to you. Because they do.

In interpersonal interactions:

- Listen more; listen better.
- Ask people about themselves, without judging.
- Let other people finish their own sentences.
- Not being "that guy" isn't enough.
- The Golden Rule 2.0: Instead of treating people the way you'd like them to treat you, treat them the way **THEY** want to be treated. (Just because you don't mind being the target of insult jokes doesn't mean other people don't mind it.)
- Believe people who've had different experiences. Just because you haven't seen something happen doesn't mean it didn't happen. Don't assume that what you need, or what you would be okay with, is what other people should accept.
- If someone says something that isn't about you, but that makes you feel defensive, stop and examine why you feel that way.
- Don't feel you need a snappy answer (or any answer) to everything.
- Don't feel you need to be right.
- Be honest, but not hurtful.
- "Yes, and…" instead of "No, but…"

(Some of these are paraphrased from responses in a Twitter thread started by Jennifer Peepas, a filmmaker and author of the advice blog Captain Awkward. Peepas asked her followers, "What would you put on a syllabus of practices to stop being an asshole?")

(Rev. Dr. Martin Luther King Jr., 1957 sermon "Loving Your Enemies"): "Hate cannot drive out hate. Only love can do that."

THE EVIL THAT DOESN'T DIE

Evil people usually don't say "I'm evil."

They more often say, "I'm so completely, innately good that I can do evil things and it's OK."

Or, they might not have a sense of "good and evil" at all.

But it doesn't ultimately matter if one does evil things out of a twisted ideology, or out of loyalty to a "tribe" (nation, ethnicity, race, religion), or just for the money, or because one's trapped in addiction or mental illness, or just because one's just following orders. The evil is still done, and it still hurts and/or kills.

(Joseph Brodsky): "What we regard as Evil is capable of a fairly ubiquitous presence if only because it tends to appear in the guise of good. You never see it crossing your threshold announcing itself: 'Hi, I'm Evil!'".... "The surest defense against Evil is extreme individualism, originality of thinking, whimsicality, even—if you will—eccentricity. That is, something that can't be feigned, faked, imitated; something even a seasoned impostor couldn't be happy with. Something, in other words, that can't be shared, like your own skin—not even by a minority."

(Mary McCarthy):"I rather agree with Kant (and always have, without knowing that Kant said it) that stupidity is caused not by brain failure, but by a wicked heart. Insensitiveness, opacity, inability to make connections, often accompanied by low 'animal' cunning. One cannot help feeling that this mental oblivion is chosen, by the heart or the moral will—an active preference, and that explains why one is so irritated by stupidity, which is not the case when one is dealing with a truly backward individual."

(John Steinbeck): "All the goodness and the heroisms will rise up again, then be cut down again and rise up. It isn't that the evil thing wins—it never will—but that it doesn't die."

(James Baldwin): "It has always been much easier (because it has always seemed much safer) to give a name to the evil without than to locate the terror within."

•

Paul Bloom's book *Against Empathy* claims "coming to experience the world as you think someone else does" (his definition of empathy) has its limits, especially with abusers and manipulators:

"It's not that empathy itself automatically leads to kindness. Rather, empathy has to connect to kindness that already exists. Empathy makes good people better, then, because kind people don't like suffering, and empathy makes this suffering salient. If you made a sadist more empathic, it would just lead to a happier sadist."

Bloom also claims "empathy is biased, pushing us in the direction of parochialism and racism," because people are tempted to only feel with people of their own type.

Instead, Bloom makes the case for "rational compassion." Bloom quotes researchers Tania Singer and Olga Klimecki on the distinction: "In contrast to empathy, compassion does not mean sharing the suffering of the other: rather, it is characterized by feelings of warmth, concern and care for the other, as well as a strong motivation to improve the other's well-being. Compassion is feeling for and not feeling with the other."

Joseph Brodsky;
Mary McCarthy.

EVERYTHING'S A STORY... 60

Many of us need to develop more empathy and/or rational compassion within, and toward, ourselves.

How? By living and relating consciously, rationally, with the head and the heart (but also with a healthy degree of awareness). A LOT easier to say than to do, I know.

(Toni Morrison, "The Source of Self-Regard"):"It is awkward to differ from a great man, but Tolstoy was wrong. Kings are not the slaves of history. History is the slave of kings.... The matrix out of which these powerful decisions are born is sometimes called racism, sometimes classism, sometimes sexism. Each is an accurate term surely, but each is also misleading. The source is a deplorable inability to project, to become the 'other,' to imagine her or him. It is an intellectual flaw, a shortening of the imagination, and reveals an ignorance of gothic proportions as well as a truly laughable lack of curiosity."

(Karen Armstrong, Twelve Steps to a Compassionate Life): "The attempt to become a compassionate being is a lifelong project. It is not achieved in an hour or a day—or even in twelve steps."

(Timothy Harris, founding director of the homeless newspaper Real Change): "Compassion, in this world, is a subversive act, and it's not for wimps. Believe it."

A hospital in my city got together with an art museum. Paintings with human figures expressing pain and suffering were shown to doctors, to help them read patients' emotions.

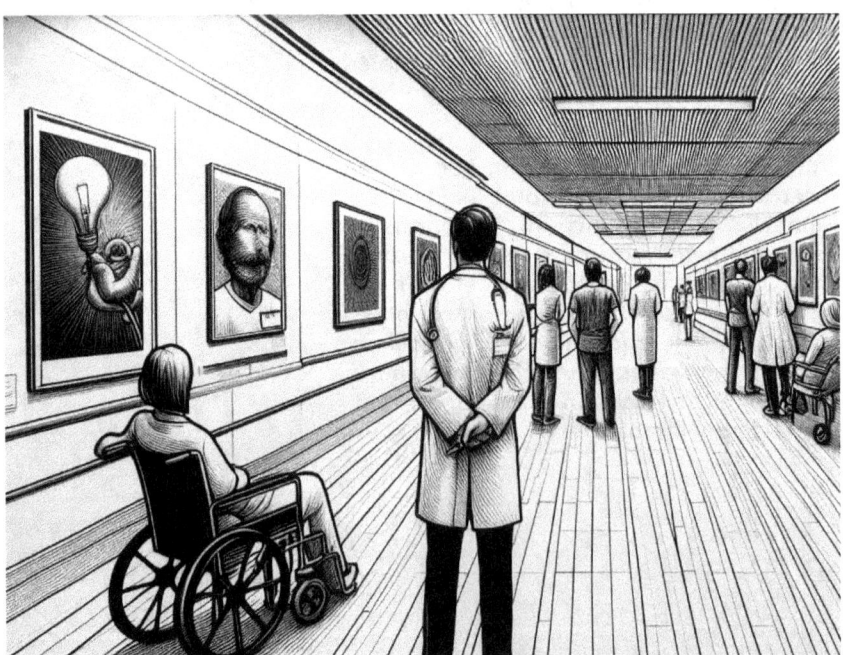

A collegiate research study showed viewing TV dramas such as *Mad Men* and *The West Wing* can "facilitate the understanding of other minds."

That study followed an earlier one that found reading literature could enhance "the ability to interpret the mental states and emotions of others." It was especially true about "literary" novels that depicted more fully-developed characters in non-formulaic plot lines.

This is "theory of mind," defined by *Psychology Today* as "*the ability to understand the thoughts, beliefs, desires, and emotions of other people.*"

Toni Morrison.

Even "big-eyes" anime, with exaggerated facial expressions, can help children who may have difficulty "reading" other people.

What it is, is the power of Story, our topic for the next several pages. (As you might have guessed by now, much of this is based on pop culture of the late 20th century, "my time.")

Storytelling is built into the psyche.

Religions are essentially stories, as are ad campaigns and computer slide presentations and social-media posts and political movements and economic theories.

Looking for "news" that's not storytelling? Stick to the stock listings and the sports statistics. (And even then, "storylines" emerge within this data and its interpretations.)

(Eric Kandel, "Theory of Mind: Why Art Evokes Empathy"): "If we see gestures in a portrait, we actually almost simulate those gestures in our mind. We often implicitly act as if we are moving our arms in response emphatically to what we see in the painting. We also respond empathically to what we think the sitter is experiencing in their head."

...BUT WHAT KIND OF STORY? 62

Many native cultures around the world didn't have written languages, and revered stories and storytelling. Not just to preserve the group's history and lore, its gods and its origin stories, but to preserve its way of thinking, its way of seeing, and therefore part of its way of life. (When the US and Canadian governments tried to make Native people assimilate into "mainstream" culture, they forced tens of thousands of children into boarding schools where the old culture was specifically banned.)

Current western culture also places an importance on stories: to sell media, to sell other stuff via marketing, to build communities and movements, to divvy people up into walled off groups, etc.

Stories have power. And that power can be used for good, or for not-so-good.

They could trap you into a "bubble" of closed-mindedness.

Or they could lead you toward something scarier but ultimately better for you.

Some stories are meant to serve to impose a false order onto the world and onto the people in it.

But some of these very same stories can be subverted, used in unintended ways, to free the mind ("...*and your ass will follow,*" as George Clinton says).

Your simplest plot structure is the NBC Chimes sequence: *Situation, Conflict, Resolution* (or the "dialectic" of *Thesis, Antithesis, Synthesis*, variously attributed to G.F.W. Hegel and Johann Fichte).

In a simple plot, there's a situation, it gets complicated, it's resolved (often but not always creating a somewhat different situation). The stolen jewels are returned. The lovers are or aren't reunited. The noble warrior heroically wins or heroically dies.

(Albert Camus):*"Fiction is the lie through which we tell the truth."*

In what we sometimes like to call "real" life, of course, not everything happens for an easily discernible reason. Events can be or seem random, or the reasons they happen are hard to figure out.

That's one reason we often prefer the worlds of stories to the so-called "real" world. They make more sense, at least to minds trained to value things that "make sense."

Some more ways to get more (fun, enlightenment, wow-factor) out of reading:

- Many neat-and-tidy-ending stories can still offer hints to a wider world, if you look for them. There are simple stories, simply told, that depict people, places, and situations that may be unfamiliar to you. Stories that can help you empathize with people, places, and situations profoundly different from your own.
- *Read for the writing, not just for the plot.* Note how you're being led along, made to care about the characters. Pay attention to the pacing: how a simple action or plot development can be written in lavish loving detail, or in quick, broad verbal "brush strokes."

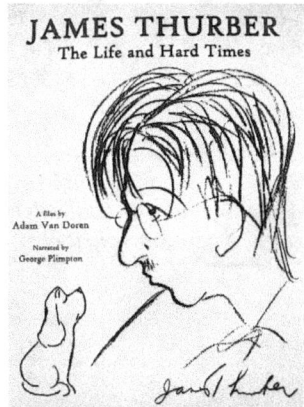

Some authors of 'simple' stories with complex meanings.

THE POWER OF PUNS   64

Some critics consider Hayao Miyazaki's Kiki's Delivery Service *to be an example of Kishotenketsu, a (relatively) conflict-free form of story.*

But there are also forms of storytelling, of story structure, that can directly expand your mind, your expectations, your sense of "reality."

Some people use the term "nonlinear narrative" to describe novels, films, video games, etc. that tell standard story arcs, but with a bunch of flashbacks and/or flash-forwards stuck into the mix—perhaps to delay resolving a mystery plot point ("why is she acting like this?," "what happened to that unseen character everybody's talking about?"). Most every murder-mystery story climaxes with a flashback (spoken and/or shown) explaining just how the victim died and by whose hand.

But more ambitious types of nonlinear storytelling attempt to make stories more like "real" life, or at least to challenge the mind's expectations.

I'm talking here about story structures that upend traditional expectations:

- Plot without conflict.
- Stories that overturn cliches of both plot tropes and character types.
- Subplots within subplots with the original base plot completely forgotten (*Tristram Shandy*).
- Heroes who turn out to be villains and vice versa.
- The ol' "unreliable narrator" trick, where you can't always trust what a character's telling you.
- Characters who die and just show up again.
- Deliberate contradictions in story or setting details; etc.

The Japanese concept of *Kishotenketsu* is a formula for a four-part storyline without conflict (the thing you're told has to go into all narrative fiction). Instead, it keeps readers/watchers interested by having the third part contain what Kate Krake calls a "contrasting, even seemingly nonsensical, departure from the character and situation set up in the first and second acts" before returning to a resolution at the end.

Also helpful to gently jar your mind: puns and aphorisms and zen koans. The short sharp shock of a sudden worldview can challenge or gently "disrupt" linear logic.

(Counter-position: Susan Sontag, who preferred the dense semiotic point of view.)

(Anne Carson, Eros the Bittersweet): "A pun is a figure of language that depends on similarity of sound and disparity of meaning. It matches two sounds that fit perfectly together as aural shapes yet stand insistently, provocatively apart in sense.... Puns appear in all literatures, are apparently as old as language and unfailingly fascinate us. Why? If we had the answer to this question we would know more clearly what the lover is searching for as he moves and reasons through the borderlands of his desire. Like Eros, puns flout the edges of things. Their power to allure and alarm derives from this. Within a pun you see the possibility of grasping a better truth, a truer meaning, than is available from the separate senses of either word. But the glimpse of that enhanced meaning, which flashes past in a pun, is a painful thing. For it is inseparable from your conviction of its impossibility. Words do have edges. So do you."

'I dropped a waffle on a California beach. Do you know what it became, my child?'

"A SANDY EGGO."

An example of Lettrist "visual poetry" using an original "typeface," by Italian artist Serse Luigetti.

Many pages back, I mentioned the Dada artists and writers, among others, as examples of depicting a healthy sense of absurdity. There are others, many others. Some examples, in various genres and forms:

- Modernism and postmodernism.
- The Lettrists, who created "visual poetry" using invented alphabets and typefaces.
- Meta fiction.
- Pataphysics.
- "Found texts," "cut-ups" (the latter popularized by William S. Burroughs).
- Magical Realism.
- Autofiction.
- The repetition in both religious texts and children's stories.
- Oulipo (a French acronym for "Workshop for Potential Literature"), who worked with self-created "constraints" to fashion new story structures. (An example: Georges Perec's novel *A Void* was written (and translated) without the letter "e.")

And this doesn't even mention the vast realms of fantasy, mythology, science fiction, and other story types that posit whole other worlds, whole other social milieux (past, present, future, or in a dimension beyond our notion of time).

But the Almighty Written Word does have its limitations; or rather, people worshiping the Almighty Written Word falsely presume it to be a universal, all-purpose savior.

There is nothing intrinsically Good about the written word or intrinsically Bad about other forms of media/expression (yes, including television).

"Books" per se don't automatically lead to enlightened or progressive attitudes.

Mein Kampf was a book.

The Protocols of the Elders of Zion was a book.

The Bell Curve was a book.

The "Sad Puppies," online trolls who virulently opposed female and minority authors winning science fiction awards, were readers, and in some cases writers, of books.

And, despite what urban left-wingers like to imagine, right-wingers DO read books. They read right-winger books. Books whose only "proof" of their theories and "realities" comes from quoting one another. Books that live in a hermetically sealed "bubble" of their own orthodoxy.

And yes, there are also left-wing books like that.

(And there are a LOT of middle-of-the-road books like that.)

A piece of "found-text poetry."

THERE GOES MY HERO

What I've said about the written word also applies to all the arts.

It certainly applies to film: from the arty and the international, to the blockbusters, to the B movies and the assembly-line "programmers" the studios used to put out to fill theater schedules.

(The whole concept of "film noir" started with French critics latching on to the best of the formula Hollywood studio thriller movies, and creating an aesthetic theory to explain their impact on audiences.)

Film, a form both extremely controlled and extremely "immersive" decades before virtual reality, can bring you so far into its experiences that you don't notice how it's working on you.

One aspect of developing a more MISCous mind is noticing how an art form is working on you. In the case of what we still call "film" (even though most modern-day feature films are shot and/or distributed as digital video), aspects you can pay special attention to include:

- Visual and sonic imagery in harmony.
- Lighting, composition, framing.
- Pacing, action/inaction, sound/silence.

George Lucas famously created the plot structure for the original *Star Wars* from professor Joseph Campbell's *The Hero's Journey* (and from the feature-length, re-edited versions of matinee adventure serials). Campbell assembled this trope from ancient myths and legends over the continents and the centuries.

"That was a GREAT thrill ride of a movie!"

"But what about the lighting, the compositions, the mise-en-scene, the sound mix...."

THE MISCosity MANIFESTO

But today, perhaps the very notion of the Hero as we know him (active, disruptive yet conformist, usually alone or in clear charge of a group, usually male, usually masculine AF) may be obsolete.

What other common story formats and shticks, past and present, might be more relevant to today?

As with any form of effective storytelling, it can let you enter the emotional lives of people different from you, from different places/times, or of people who could be your own acquaintances.

And, as with any form of effective "spectacle," it can be a mind-changing and experience-enhancing thang on its own.

As one example, think of low-budget, over-the-top action movies, not as "so bad they're good" but as works of garage-rock style, lo-fi, unbridled enthusiasm.

As another example, explore certain films that examine/question the nature of "reality" itself, such as *Solaris* and *2001*. (What, you thought I was going to say *The Matrix*?)

Then there's the vast range of non-narrative film, roughly defined as moving pictures that don't tell a linear plot. The films that are most often called "art" works. (But aren't they all?)

•

The cinema took and still takes "inspiration" from anything and everything—literature and comics, and also poetry and painting. But its principal influence, particularly in the early "talkie" era, was live theater.

STAGES OF LIFE

Yiddish theater and vaudeville: two of the building blocks of the American stage.

Theatrical performance is an in-person experience that can do things that an experience that's canned and up on a screen can't do. It's right there with you (in your literal "face"). And the stage is not bound by film's ingrained obsession with detail and hyper-realism.

The US theater scene is crippled (still) by the idea that something created on an island off the Atlantic coast is "national," while something created on the North American mainland is merely "regional," destined at best to feed its best scripts and people to Manhattan and get back bus-and-truck touring productions in return.

No. Real theater, like all the best in all the arts, can come from anyone and anywhere.

Especially during my lifetime, since the Ford Foundation started seed-funding professional theater organizations across the mainland US in 1961-62.

Yet even the Manhattan theater world was never a sealed bubble.

It relied on the whole NYC ethnic "melting pot" of influences, from European immigrants (Irish, Italian, eastern European, Jewish-from-wherever), from African Americans migrating northward; and also on input from openly and almost-openly gay men, from women as creators as well as performers, from the ethnic and gender and class struggles (to the extent that "the market" and local censors allowed), from other art forms (Hollywood films, jazz, rock n' roll), and from theater works born in the UK and Europe.

Partly because it wasn't "in the can" like films, and thus dependent on amassing the largest possible revenue from each production, live performance could and does take innumerable forms and formats. Some of the more innovative ones:

- The Little Theater Movement; the Living Newspaper; the avant-garde theater of Europe; expressionism and absurdism.
- Conceptual and performance art.
- Sketch comedy (Nichols & May, the original Second City).

Some more types of stage works, of the "legitimate theater" variety and otherwise, that can bring MISCosity:

- Ol' Willie the S. Himself wrote 37 plays, most of which can still tell us a lot about human nature's potentials and limitations (I'll forgive you if you skip the obscurities like *Pericles, Prince of Tyre*). Modern productions of his plays have the added enhancement of female roles portrayed by what we now call "cis" females! (Even more recently: productions with *male* roles portrayed by "cis" females!)
- The old Greeks had a lot of staying power in some of their words and their worlds.
- And so do a lot of other national and international traditions: Japanese *noh* and *kabuki*, Euro-Christian passion and mystery plays, African and Native American mythological performance. A lot of these forms rely less on "people standing around talking," and more on the more universal languages of movement, music, costume, and audience interaction.

THE REST OF THE GLOBE THEATER

NOW PLAYING

BUTOH
KABUKI
ZULU TRIBAL DANCE
GREEK TRAGEDY
CHINESE OPERA
HUNGARIAN OPERETTA
MYSTERY PLAYS
SHADOW PUPPETRY
COMMEDIA DELL'ARTE
ENGLISH PANTOS
HAPPENINGS
PERFORMANCE ART
IMPROV

DANCE ME TO THE END OF LOVE 72

The dance as interpreted by Jules Feiffer and Martha Graham; operatic bombast updated.

The dance is the one art form at which women were traditionally allowed to be prominent, at least in some places (Japan's traditionally all-male *noh* among the exceptions). Martha Graham, Isadora Duncan, and Twyla Tharp are but some of the medium's leading lights.

Dance, as abstracted and codified human movement, exists in most every nation and culture. It tells stories and legends, new and old. It expresses the full gamut of character and emotion, of action and interaction, of individuals and societies, without uttering a word.

The same goes for narrative musical works.

Even opera, despite its bombast and its penchant for "cultural appropriation" (and, oh yeah, for the "strong women" in them almost always dying in the end), can transport you into a made-up realm of big feelings and subtle shifts in tone. Richard Wagner's *The Ring of the Nibelung* (14 hours in four segments) tells of gods and demons and material-lust and sex-lust and a lot of stuff that more or less got into *The Lord of the Rings* (except for the sex aspects of course). Composers and authors are still creating new major works in the opera form, with such larger-than-life subjects as Richard Nixon and Jerry Springer.

THE MISCosity MANIFESTO

Animation is its own art form, within but mostly outside the corporate colossus known as "Disney." The Zoetrope and the flip book predate the invention of film, so animation technically preceded live action cinema. Such silent-era works as Windsor McCay's *Gertie the Dinosaur* and the Fleischer brothers' *Out of the Inkwell* series did with composition, characterization, and timing what mere sequential photographs of human actors couldn't and still can't.

But the theatrical "cartoon" became a stepchild of the Hollywood studio system, with limited budgets, tight production schedules, and formulaic contents.

Despite (or more likely because of) these disciplines, many seven-minute gems emerged. Such masterworks as Tex Avery's *Red Hot Riding Hood* and Chuck Jones's *One Froggy Evening* remain more beloved and more "current" than many of the live-action feature films with which they were originally screened.

Further examples from the world of animation:

- Abstract animation (Oskar Rishinger, Norman McLaren, Harry Smith, Len Lye, others).

- National Film Board of Canada animation, from the gentle nostalgia of *The Hockey Sweater* to the nihilistic absurdity of *The Big Snit*.

- Central/Eastern European animation, with its own takes on character design, gag pacing, and minimized dialogue for the sake of easy international distribution.

- The real "lesson" of 1980s "educational" cartoons: quality doesn't matter, as long as it's under budget and meets bureaucratic requirements.

DRAWING THE LINE

Comics, or comix, or "co-mix" (a "retronym" term coined in the 1970s I believe), is an art form combining text, imagery, linear (or non-linear or multi-linear) narrative, and the ubiquitous but under-appreciated art of graphic design (more on that in a few pages), to do more than any one of those can do alone.

"Sequential art" is as old as cave paintings. It's enshrined in churches (the Catholics' "stations of the cross") and Chinese scrolls.

In North America, it became a major part of the golden age of newspapers (with the likes of *Little Nemo, Popeye, Li'l Abner, Krazy Kat, The Spirit, Peanuts, Pogo, The Far Side*), then a stepchild to the magazine industry that still generated works of lasting value (*Uncle $crooge, Sugar and Spike, Herbie*, EC's horror comics).

France and Belgium's "graphic albums" (*bandes desinée*) and Japan's manga offered book-length narratives intended for a variety of audiences in a variety of genres.

In 1960s-70s America, "underground comix" indulged overtly in sex and drugs (but, strangely, not in rock n' roll much), but also opened new opportunities for creators through small publishers and specialty retailers. From that grew "alternative" comics (including, among my faves, the Hernandez brothers' *Love and Rockets*), and eventually the graphic novel explosion.

Comics have been called a "frozen cinema," using sequential visuals and dialogue/narration (only without music, sound, actors, elapsed time, or motion).

What comics do have that cinema (usually) doesn't: the juxtaposition of imagery and text, pacing, showing vs. telling, realism vs. caricature, and much more. (See Scott McCloud's book *Understanding Comics* for the whole fascinating story.)

by Jerry Robinson

THE MISCosity MANIFESTO

We've mentioned how music and math (and, therefore, the universe) are intricately connected. ("The music of the spheres," as it were.)

Music can directly "re-tune" your brain to other ways of perception; especially "outré" or avant garde music (utilizing dissonance, atonalities, alternate keys and time signatures). It's enough of a known fact that whole companies built themselves around it, such as the workplace-music company Muzak with its concepts of "stimulus progression" to keep workers productive.

Some examples:

- Charles Ives' deliberate sonic chaos.
- John Cage's "prepared" instruments (also explored by, of all people, piano duo Ferrante & Teicher in their pre-orchestral-kitsch years).

I loved milieux where you could see or hear any music juxtaposed to most any other, as long as it fit under one arbitrary label. "Top 40" radio played any song (within FCC language rules) that happened to sell a lot of 45s. Dolly Parton, Lynyrd Skynyrd, Bob Dylan, and Suzy Quatro could appear in a single on-air set. *The Dr. Demento Show*, a syndicated Sunday-night radio series, played any type of song (again, within FCC rules) whose words were funny.

(Schopenhauer): "*The composer reveals the innermost nature of the world, and expresses the profoundest wisdom, in a language that his reasoning faculty does not understand.*"

BEHIND THE MUSIC   76

Music of any genre can help to rewire your brain, especially music of a genre unfamiliar to you.

In particular, seek out the music with the "roll" as well as the "rock." The "real thing" (ragtime, bebop, R&B), not the soggy and sweetened up (or loud and dumbed down) (but usually white) "mainstream" or "retro" versions.

Why R&B revival acts often seem phony: it's not just that they're not Black, so much as they're not "blue." The James Brown horn section could play perfectly AND play "human," with that subtle touch of emotional honesty that simple aggression can't copy.

Examine why some music turns some people on and other people off. Punk rock was originally deemed "harsh and abrasive" by old fogeys (political conservatives) and old hippies (aesthetic conservatives) alike, and yet was "reassuring" to its listeners, its converts, the lonely people in rural/suburban Earth seeking a message that "it gets better." Even if the message was embedded within the cultural aesthetic of Lou Reed and Joey Ramone's Manhattan lowlife, or Henry Rollins and Exene Cervenka's Los Angeles nihilism.

And try listening closely to obscure music and music not meant to be listened to closely: industrial/background music, production library tracks, soundtrack cues, album filler tracks and single B-sides, obscure regional and local releases.

The history of music can teach a lot about the specific times and places of its making.

Among the many examples: Black contributions to early country music (including DeFord Bailey, left), which at one point was nearly indistinguishable from "race music," became forgotten as the country genre became "bleached" due to the Grand Ole Opry's casting policies, Henry Ford's campaign to publicize an institutionalized version of square dancing, etc.

THE MISCosity MANIFESTO

Periodicals, as much as music, are an art form for "the masses"– yes, even those periodicals officially meant, as so many in recent decades were, for an "upscale demographic."

The magazine is a "happy medium" between the newspaper's relentless daily deadlines and the book's one-shot nature. It provides a regular, reassuring visit into a virtual realm where a specific range of topics is addressed in a specific verbal and visual manner.

Marshall McLuhan and his disciples noted the various revolutions that came from Johannes Gutenberg's printed Bibles: the penny press, mass magazines, tabloid newspapers, revolutionary fliers such as the American Thomas Paine's *Common Sense*, a Kansas leftist publisher's *Little Blue Book* pamphlets, hippie underground newspapers and comix, photocopied zines, self-published print-on-demand books.

This entrepreneurial spirit spread to other media with 45s, cassettes, spoken-word political cassettes (particularly in the old Warsaw Pact countries and Iran), CD-Rs, VCRs, DVDs, streaming, blogs, vlogs, and podcasts.

Collage by oldmagazinearticles.com.

DESIGN FOR LIVING 78

Graphic design may be the most ubiquitous (and therefore least noticed) commercial culture form of them all, as my onetime colleague Art Chantry wrote in his book simply titled *Art Chantry Speaks*.

Personal computers have taught millions about the intricacies of typography (what the more casual users call "fonts").

That's only one of the most obvious aspects of a commercial art that encompasses industrial history (movable type, "hot type," "cold type," "desktop publishing"), aesthetic evolution (the early *New Yorker's* preppy preciousness, the early *Life's* love of "white space"), marketing theory (those 1970s fashion-ad drawings of women with five-foot-tall legs and two-foot-tall torsos), political theory (how Italian futurists influenced the fascists), and so much more.

Graphic design puts text, imagery, and text-as-imagery into a finely-tuned mesh, that not only tells us things but tells us how to view what we're told.

THE MISCosity MANIFESTO

Visual art, as hinted at earlier in this chapter, makes the viewer stand still and notice the details, something needed in our often hyper-paced world.

It's useful for seeing what other people in other places/times saw as beautiful, or inspirational, or morally uplifting, or instructive, or the stories they felt needed telling.

Historian and BBC host Sir Kenneth Clark used art to reveal different times/places' notions of "the Ideal" in forms, shapes, compositions, color schemes, and people.

From the early 20th century on (with Dada, Fluxus, futurism, cubism, constructivism, et al.), modern artists disrupted the notion that visual art should be (1) "beautiful," (2) "realistic," or even (3) comprehensible.

By the 1950s, the US government secretly funded "modern art" in many forms and formats, as a Cold War strategy to win intellectual hearts and minds away from the Soviets (whose official artistic tastes, after a few early experimental years, had settled toward plodding, mind-numbing "socialist realism").

But the many flavors of modern and postmodern art were hardly the first movements in art history to challenge, or play tricks with, their viewers. Previous centuries saw painters and illustrators dealing in forced perspective, anamorphosis* (wide images "squeezed" into narrow spaces), tricks of position, marginalia, hidden objects.

*(The widescreen film process CinemaScope was "anamorphic" in that it used special lenses to squeeze a wide image onto standard 35mm film. The original *101 Dalmatians* is a CinemaScope film with funny animal characters, which makes it both "anamorphic" and "anthropomorphic.")

ON THE WALLS; OFF THE WALL

Many works, genres, and movements in the arts come with attached philosophical explanations.

Especially in the visual arts.

These explanations can be as brief as the traditional "artist's statement" posted at a gallery or museum exhibit (a genre of its own), and as long as entire books and college courses.

Sometimes these explanations come from the artists themselves; sometimes they come from critics and analysts.

Sometimes, the art works made within these movements serve primarily as "proofs of concept" for the philosophy.

One example is the Pre-Raphaelites, a close-knit group of Brits who wanted to bring back classical painting methods as a means toward reclaiming old aesthetic values (and, by extension, old societal values).

But the concept of tying visual art, with its immediate sensual impact, to long verbal statements really took off in the early 20th century with the umpteen modern (and later, post-modern) sub-genres.

The Dada artists toyed with both the verbal and the visual, issuing "artist statements" as playfully yet seriously absurd as their paintings and sculptures.

Later modern and postmodern movements, from the reactionary to the revolutionary, from the brashly modern to the introspectively postmodern, issued statements (or had statements issued on their behalf) that tended to bury the art's immediate impact beneath heavy pontification on The Self vs. The Other, or The Subject vs. The Signifier, or that eternally-popular topic of Gender Roles.

THE MISCosity MANIFESTO

You can enjoy an art work without reading their justifications or interpretations. Or you can immerse yourself in the words that go with them.

Some 19th and 20th Century art movement ideas (way over-simplified and in non-chronological order):

- Cubism: Angular components, African-inspired.
- Futurism: Industrial-age speed and power.
- Impressionism: Away from accurate representation, toward emotional impact,
- Expressionism: Emotional impact, not visual accuracy.
- *De Stijl*: Total geometric abstraction; representing only itself.
- Depression Realism: Everyday lives of quiet despair.
- Fauvism: Big brushstrokes on big canvases.
- Surrealism: Symbolic fantasy; dreamscapes.
- Pop Art: Art-ifying the iconography of celebrities and merchandise.
- Op Art: Optical illusions (and allusions) that "move" while staying still.

Pastiches of the styles of cubism, impressionism, Depression realism, and pop art.

THE STATES OF THE ART; THE ART OF THE STATE

Aesthetic-social critic Susan Sontag wrote many books about the arts and how to view them.

But in her book *Against Interpretation*, she warned against over-analyzing "texts" (and other creative works) to the point where they're construed to mean things their creators never intended.

Sontag also believed that some forms of interpretation negate the aesthetic and sensual impact of a work, by reducing it to mere "content": *"Real art has the capacity to make us nervous. By reducing the work of art to its content and then interpreting that, one tames the work of art. Interpretation makes art manageable, conformable.... Interpretation, based on the highly dubious theory that a work of art is composed of items of content, violates art. It makes art into an article for use, for arrangement into a mental scheme of categories."*

Sontag called interpretation "the revenge of intellectualism against the world."

Interpretation, along with the related routines of analysis and "deconstruction," became major building blocks of "postmodern" art, a loosely-connected set of genres and disciplines.

French philosopher Jacques Derrida, a chief promoter of 'deconstruction' as applied to language and writing.

To grossly oversimplify it (and yes, I've been engaging in gross oversimplification all through this), postmodernism begins with the premise "after modern art, then what?"

To many artists, the "then what" answer included varying proportions of previous genres and disciplines, all mixed-n'-matched. Full-room installation pieces could include careful arrangements of everything from found objects to elaborate abstract works. Performance art could include everything from free-verse poetry and musical samples to large-group choreography and audience participation. Characters, plot premises, and imagery were borrowed from the world over.

The mixing-n'-matching can be worthwhile, and in some instances is terrific. It helps show how every culture and age has things to teach us. When done unthinkingly, though, it can just rehash old stereotypes about one's capital-O "Others." Or worse, it can lead to embarrassing "cultural appropriation," as in the case of the white male painter who submitted works to competitions under the name of a Black woman, then hired an actress to portray the pseudonym at panel discussions, all as part of a "project."

But the broad swatch of "postmodern" also includes a lot of interpretation, in various forms: from verbose "semiotic" analysis to works that don't get very far beyond "deconstructing" previous works, aesthetics, or statements.

Perpetual "deconstruction" sometimes feels the same as the tech bros' obsession with "disruption," in which whole established industries are turned into shambles, not really to build something better but just to make a few guys richer. Other times it feels the same as saying everything with the "air quotes" of detached insincerity.

We don't need more one-dimensional statements about how commercial Squaresville culture (fashion ads, porn, TV, pop music) is too one-dimensional.

GETTING FREE BY GETTING 'STUCK' 84

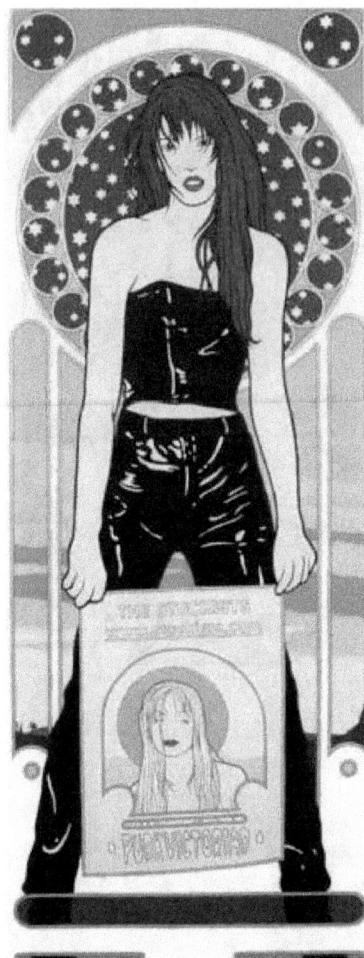

'The Stuckists Punk Victorian,' exhibit poster by Paul Harvey, 2004.

In aesthetics, as in politics, you need to show an alternative to what you say you're against.

There are recent movements in the arts that try to bring back sincerity, "agency," and the fierce need to Do Something for the World.

Metamodernism, which we've already discussed, is one of them.

There are also Stuckism and Remodernism, related concepts championed by musician/artist Billy Childish and partner Charles Thompson. Wikipedia says the joint movement "...*aims to get back to the true spirit of modernism, to produce art with spiritual value regardless of style, subject matter or medium.*"

In other words: if you're going to do something, *mean it*.

(UC Berkeley art prof Kevin Radley on Remodernism): "*...A renewal of artists working without the limitation of irony and cynicism... a renewal of the sense of beauty.*"

(David Foster Wallace): "*Irony and cynicism were just what the US hypocrisy of the fifties and sixties called for. That's what made the early postmodernists great artists.... The problem is that once the rules of art are debunked, and once the unpleasant realities the irony diagnoses are revealed and diagnosed, 'then' what do we do? Irony's useful for debunking illusions, but most of the illusion-debunking in the US has now been done and redone.*"

Video games are also an art form—and not just the ones like *Minecraft* that offer online tools for creating on-screen landscapes and cityscapes, or the ones like *Cuphead* that call back to 1920s-30s cartooning, or the ones like *Myst* that tell different sides of what's ultimately a linear narrative.

The best ones, the "stickiest ones," immerse players in "worlds" with boundaries and rules. Even if those boundaries are as small as the maze in *Pac-Man* or as big as the realms of *Second Life* and *World of Warcraft*.

There are even games "that made people question their beliefs," by putting them in the virtual shoes of their "Others" (or of fictional characters reminiscent of their "Others").

A 2019 article on *Kotaku.com*, "The Video Games That Made People Question Their Beliefs," mentions a Mormon Republican from Salt Lake City who'd enjoyed the 2005 Nintendo-published game *Fire Emblem: Path of Radiance*, in which defenders of the fictional nation of "Crimea" drive out invaders from "Daein." But then he played its sequel, *Radiant Dawn*, played from the POV of Daein resistance fighters when their own country is occupied. This was while "the Iraq War was in full swing," and "he hadn't really considered the humanity of the Iraqi people... But *Radiant Dawn* forced him to think about what it would be like to live in an occupied country."

THE NOT-SO-'IDIOT' BOX

For more than a half century before the "new golden age" of the medium, TV was the consummation of all the entertainment, information, and arts genres developed to date. TV was influenced by (and influenced) the conventions and formats of cinema, theater, radio, music, dance, newspapers, magazines, short stories, novels, graphic design, animation, comics, and more.

When TV showed up it was, even more than radio and movies had been, a "tube" that collected input from all the world's pop-cultural heritage (music, drama, comedy, monologue and dialogue, speeches and sermons, documentary, sports, newsreels, fashion, graphic design, animation, clowning/puppetry, etc.). In other countries, and in the US once NET/PBS got going, the highbrow arts got added into the mix ("art" film, classical music and opera, dance, "high" drama).

The result: NOT a simple "dumbing down of everything" (or at least not just that). Rather, a great (and continuing) cross-influencing and cross-pollinating.

The Twilight Zone, Star Trek, and *Doctor Who* brought new generations of fans into the wider worlds of sci-fi/fantasy/horror.

MTV, in its "Music Television" early years, exposed millions to pop, rock, and rap acts they couldn't hear on local radio. The music video genre can be seen as a thousand brief lessons in non-linear visual storytelling.

A feature film runs between 70 and 180 minutes, and includes as much or as little "story" as can fit. Directors and screenwriters developed all sorts of shortening and stretching shticks to make narratives fit the allotted time. TV and video, especially in the streaming era, can tell a "story" as short as 10 seconds and as long as 100 hours (in the case of *telenovelas*).

TV's content limitations were historically even more market-concentrated than those of film, because channels were controlled by major institutions (advertisers and corporations in this country, governments in many other countries).

Yet many substantive and even socially questioning works have come out of it, in so many places. Sometimes these messages had to be couched in metaphor or historical parallels, just as films and novels had to do at various places and times. So you had '60s sitcoms (that most commercial and "timeless" of all TV genres) where various "Others" tried to fit into suburban (read: white) conformity (*Bewitched*) or gleefully didn't try (*The Addams Family*), and where women pushed the boundaries of the "good little housewife" (*I Love Lucy, I Dream of Jeannie*). If you couldn't criticize big business predations in present-day stories, you could have the *Little House on the Prairie* people blow up their town before greedy new landowners took it over.

In the Museum of Broadcast Communications in Chicago in 1988, I watched two 30-ish men staring at a videotape of a long-gone local kids' show, rapt in their own pasts from images and sounds that meant nothing to me.

This was long before YouTube, whose many uses include the dredging up of media heritages.

Now, uncountable representative samples of the past century-plus of TV, radio, records, movies, live performance, and anything else involving pictures, sounds, and/or words is only a few clicks away; much of it for free (after the cost of the viewing/listening device and of the online connection).

BLOGS AND VLOGS AND TUBERS   **88**

If the main (among some critics) complaint about television was that it was a few-to-many medium controlled by either advertisers and/or governments (depending on the country in which you lived), streaming video is open to anyone with a smartphone, a laptop, and basic editing software. And for more than just "influencers" plugging consumer products. "Vloggers" and "YouTubers" are among the top new DIY media creators.

So are podcasters (both audio and video varieties). They're direct communicators, without even the middlemen of stations and (in many cases) sponsors. Anyone can say anything, censored only by streaming providers' "community guidelines." You don't need a business model if you're putting it out for free.

That has naturally led to home movies put up for all to see but not intended for mass viewing; conspiracy theories; preaching; ads for the video-makers' products; homemade sex tapes (on specialty "sex tube" sites); and death threats against women and minorities who want to increase diversity in science fiction and video games.

But it's also led to a revival of audio drama; new forms of short- and long-form audio/video documentaries; a revival of experimental/art filmmaking.

(While podcasts have had a massive creative spurt, traditional radio has calcified into talk show hosts spurting bigoted insults as "outrage porn"; "public" radio programs smugly persuading affluent listeners to feel good about themselves; and highly restrictive music formats built around advertisers' demographic targets.)

As we've seen, the arts in all their "brow" levels (high, low, furrowed) raise issues about the meaning of life and reality.

Especially when these forms and means are changing so quickly, so completely.

Marshall McLuhan was famous for popularizing media studies with catch phrases such as "The Medium Is the Message" (later followed up with his book title *The Medium Is the Massage*).

McLuhan proclaimed (in a low-key, very Canadian manner) that the way a mass medium operates has as much impact on citizens as a medium's content. TV is a warm glow, like listening to stories at a campfire. Theatrical cinema is both seductive and in your face at the same time. Magazines, and the colorful ads within them, presaged TV in creating "brand narratives," etc.

Later critics such as Jerry Mander over-simplified McLuhan's lessons into one-dimensional rants (Books = *Good!* TV = *Bad!*).

This one-dimensional approach proved popular among certain American males who couldn't stop boasting that they hadn't watched television in X number of years—and who often dismissed those who did enjoy the small screen as an undifferentiated mass of passive, mind-controlled "sheeple."

IT'S SO SPECTACLE-ULAR!

Still another approach was taken by Guy Debord, one of the French Situationists, in his book *Society of the Spectacle*. Riffing off the opening of Marx's *Das Kapital*, Debord wrote: "In societies where modern conditions of production prevail, all of life presents itself as an immense accumulation of spectacles. Everything that was directly lived has moved away into representation."

Since his day, one could argue that online and social media have taken this process a lot further.

Even before the rise of social media or a dozen streaming TV services each with its own exclusive shows, we were already smack dab within a post-mass media landscape.

In a 2007 essay, the aforementioned David Foster Wallace described this immersive environment as "... *a kind of Total Noise that's also the sound of our US culture right now, a culture and volume of info and spin and rhetoric and context that I know I'm not alone in finding too much to even absorb, much less to try to make sense of or organize into any kind of triage of saliency or value. Such basic absorption, organization, and triage used to be what was required of an educated adult, a.k.a. an informed citizen—at least that's what I got taught. Suffice it here to say that the requirements now seem different.*"

•

The need for a more MISCous aesthetic is no more true than in the art form we all carry around upon us, fashion.

And where you have talk about fashion images these days, you'll also find talk about body image issues, and girls and women who torture themselves (mentally, and by physical means such as starvation) to achieve a "look" they don't already have.

THE MISCosity MANIFESTO

The vast majority of people don't have fashion-model figures. If you don't believe me, just go to any public beach in the summertime.

Real human bodies come in all shapes, all colors, all sizes.

And, in MISCosity, all of these are equally all right.

So why does the clothing biz seem to believe otherwise?

Naomi Wolf's 1990 book *The Beauty Myth* condemned the fashion industry and the mass media for spreading unrealistic standards of physical beauty.

And as more women have gained more power in society and in the workplace, the pressure to conform to those standards hasn't shrunk but grown.

Wolf and other critics also find the fashion industry to be full of negativity toward its own customers.

Yet at least superficially, fashion marketing is all positive.
Unrelentingly (even toxically) positive.

In these fantasy worlds, every person's young and thin and rich (but doesn't have to, you know, work). She has fabulous friends. She goes to the coolest places in the world. She has great adventures day and night, while always looking completely perfect.

She wears the latest styles, that only really look good on people who look just like she does.

THE BEAUTY IN MEGA-DIVERSITY

(Andy Warhol in Andy Warhol: A Documentary Film (2006), *talking with New York male fashion models):* "You're the only people these clothes look good on. And you don't wear them in real life."

You don't have to let commercial forces order you to want what they want you to want.

But it's still OK to view, read, and partake of these fantasies.

As long as you know they are fantasies, with little relation to reality.

(Although some of my left-wing friends would say it's never good to idolize the idle rich.)

But don't settle for exchanging one impossible, universal ideal with another.

Don't go, "That's not how everybody everywhere should look; *this* is."

That would be too much like the fashion industry's "planned obsolescence."

And it would be just as stifling.

Clothes, styles, and looks need to be just as MISCous as people are.

Since there are as many different "genders" and sexualities as there are people, there should also be as many "looks" as there are people.

For some, less flashy and more practical.

For others, less drab and more outrageous. ("Cosplay," every day.)

What would fashion look like in a more healed society?

What would fashion-model videos sound like in a more healed society? Would the endless repetition of the same Katy Perry and Portishead songs give way to the models' brief monologues about philosophical theories?

Black, Latinx, and Asian American activists have often dressed for respect, visually demanding to be treated with dignity. They were reaching for the social status that many '60s-'70s white baby boomers tried, at least temporarily, to escape from.

What is "sexy"?

What is "manly," "womanly"?

Indeed, what is "beauty"?

Some philosophers tried to concoct a concrete, "objective" definition.

But a more MISCosity-based view would say "it depends."

Specifically, the idea/ideal of beauty depends on place, time, subculture, and infinite other factors.

Over the centuries and the nations, there have been countless different ideals of beauty, both in human figures and in the larger world.

But everywhere, women and men have honed and refined their outward appearance.

To identify with a culture or subculture ("mainstream," "alternative," and all gradations in between).

To express an individual aesthetic.

THE RUN FOR THE 'ROSES'

Human cultures, modern and ancient, all over the world, have fashioned their visual appearance. There will always be the ideal of beauty, in one's person and in one's surroundings. What forms that ideal will take in the future remain a great adventure.

A song popularized by suffragettes and female labor leaders in the early 20th Century went, "Give us bread, but give us roses."

'Hearts starve as well as bodies. Give us bread, but give us roses.'

The "bread," of course, signified material needs.

The "roses" officially signified the equal need for women's dignity and respect.

But, interpreted differently, it could also mean that human life needs aesthetics, beauty, the senses, the traditionally *yin* approach to life.

Euclid tried to put beauty down into equations, including the Golden Ratio and the Golden Rectangle.

It ties in with everything, as everything does.

There is beauty in Order (the "fearful symmetry" in William Blake's poem *The Tyger*).

But there is also beauty, often an even greater beauty, in Chaos (or the seeming Chaos), in randomness (or the seeming randomness), in complexity, in diversity, in the unexpected and the unplanned.

If you know how to look for it.

Indeed, one way to tell the difference between true "chaos" and the "seemingly-random complexity" we lauded toward this book's start is the ease at which you can find beauty in it. Art and entertainment works that are merely chaotic don't have enough sense of craft, of mastery, of the makers knowing what they're doing.

Artists have looked for (and found) beauty in the seemingly chaotic, including composer John Cage and painter Jackson Pollack.

This is NOT to say everything needs to conform to some standard of "quality" or "good taste." In many ways, something "tasteful" and orderly can be a crashing bore; while something seemingly disordered or ineptly crafted (but made with heart and soul behind it) can radiate its own beauty. The films of Edward D. Wood Jr. and the works of many "untaught" painters have shown this.

(John Keats, "Ode on a Grecian Urn"):"Beauty is truth; truth, beauty."

(Fyodor Dostoevsky, The Idiot)*:"Beauty will save the world."*

(Marshall McLuhan, The Medium Is the Massage)*: "There's a wonderful sign hanging in a Toronto junkyard which reads, 'Help Beautify Junkyards. Throw Something Lovely Away Today.'"*

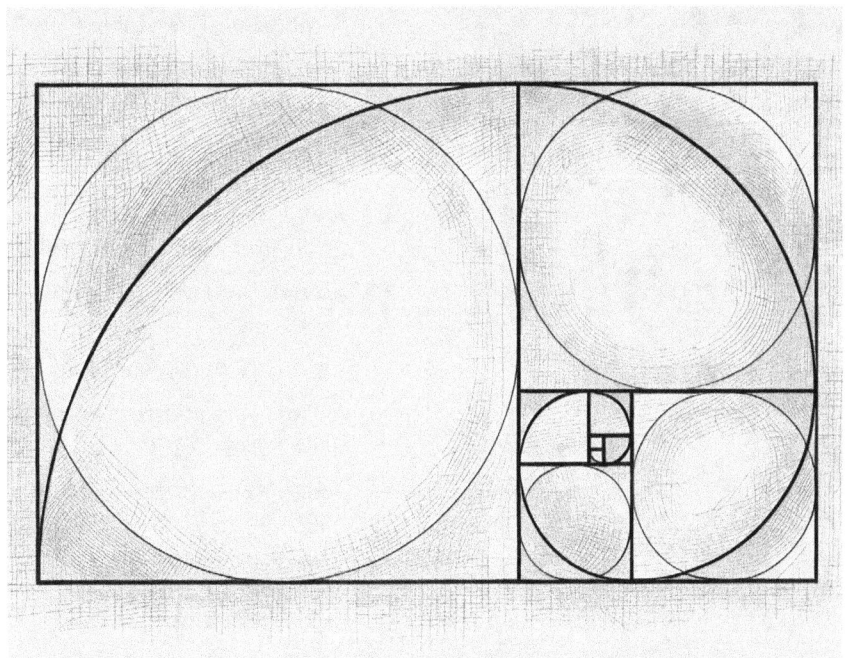

A rendering of the Golden Ratio, based on a design by Freepik.com.

A THING (WELL, MANY THINGS) OF BEAUTY

Things that can contain beauty:

The great outdoors.

- A meadow.
- A waterfall.
- A mountain range.
- A desert.
- A rainstorm.
- The day and night skies and everything in between.

Works of art and craft.

- A painting, drawing, engraving, sculpture, installation piece, photo, cartoon, etc.
- A garment, on its own or well-modeled.
- A meal, and its place setting.
- A film, video, animation, etc.
- A piece of music, "found sound," etc.
- A classic newspaper front page, magazine layout, etc.
- A novel, poem, aphorism, essay, etc.

Works of industry and technology.

- A gleaming sports car; a rusted pickup truck.
- A factory; a piece of factory equipment.
- A modern personal computer or smartphone; a computer chip.

THE MISCosity MANIFESTO

The "built environment."
- A factory.
- A house.
- An apartment, and an apartment building.
- A city street; a country road; the long lonesome highway.

An organism, from an amoeba to a human and beyond.

A human emotion.

A human soul.

An idea.

Works of science.

A "fractal" art work (derived from an equation that may contain random factors but isn't "chaotic").

An equation ("$E=mc^2$" has often been described as "a work of beauty").

A passage of software code.

•

Beauty is the antidote to the anti-aesthetic of much modern corporate society.

What's uglier than a suburban office-park and strip-mall streetscape that seems to know it's ugly and doesn't care?

It never had to be that way. And it still doesn't.

Some architects and design activists around the world have proposed new, attractive AND functional remodels to (or replacements for) derelict strip malls.

THE KITSCH NICHE

Zadie Smith; Elaine Scarry; William Butler Yeats.

Big-box stores could have an aesthetic purpose to them, as the now-defunct Best Products chain proved. Even concrete-slab "brutalist" architecture has a few examples worth championing.

Zadie Smith's 1985 novel *On Beauty* weaves its many themes of race/gender identity through its tale of a black woman teaching at an elite northeast US college. One of these themes is beauty, in some of its many forms and concepts, including human physical beauty (with and without a specifically sexual aspect). Some of her characters have, and overcome, body image issues, to recognize their own external and/or internal beauty.

Smith took her title from Harvard prof Elaine Scarry's 1998 essay *On Beauty and Being Just*. Its arguments make a case toward the ideal of bringing more traditionally feminine concepts into greater social influence, re-balancing the *yin* and the *yang*.

Still another notion of beauty is invoked in William Butler Yeats's poem *Easter 1916*, with its repeating refrain *"A terrible beauty is born."* The poem's about the Irish independence movement of the early 20th century. Yeats saw it as a magnificent change for the Irish people, though one achieved at a very bloody cost. Beauty can be found within terror, and vice versa.

Because we will need to make early 21st century neo-fascism not just defeated but passé, we need an aesthetic of beauty for a new age.

One that champions the beauty in ultra-diversity.

Milan Kundera's novel *The Unbearable Lightness of Being* (set during the brief "Prague Spring" of 1968 and the subsequent Soviet invasion of Czechoslovakia) states that *"...behind Communism, Fascism, behind all occupations and invasions lurks a more basic, pervasive evil and that the image of that evil was a parade of people marching by with raised fists and shouting identical syllables in unison."*

The novel includes long passages about the nature of "kitsch," less in the term's artistic meaning (excess sentimentality and melodramatics) than in its aesthetic meaning.

To Kundera, kitsch represents a world *"in which shit is denied and everyone acts as though it did not exist.... Kitsch excludes everything from its purview which is essentially unacceptable in human existence."*

Kundera invoked "kitsch" to denounce both ludicrous Nazi pomposity and lifeless Soviet brutalism. Kundera wrote that the paintings, posters, and architecture produced under these aesthetics were worse than banal; they aimed to shut down people's sensibilities, to kill the human imagination.

In political and social mores, Kundera calls kitsch *"the aesthetic ideal of all politicians and all political parties and movements."*

At its extreme level is "totalitarian kitsch," in which *"everything that infringes on kitsch must be banished for life: every display of individualism (because a deviation from the collective is a spit in the eye of the smiling brotherhood); every doubt (because anyone who starts doubting details will end by doubting life itself); all irony (because in the realm of kitsch everything must be taken quite seriously)."*

BAD CAMP VS. GOOD CAMP

You should also be wary of some other modern variants on kitsch.

One is kitsch consumed "ironically," by laughing (out loud or silently) at everyone else who's supposedly consuming it. Kundera implied irony was something "totalitarian kitsch" opposed, but late-20th and 21st century American kitsch feeds on it as an excuse.

In the late 1980s and 1990s, I saw, and came to loathe, this kind of "hip" superior attitude, the "so bad it's good" attitude.

Among the objects of this ridicule: wrestling, supermarket tabloids, celebrity gossip, televangelists, the nascent genre of "reality TV," campy '50s-'60s movies, "trashy" paperback novels, conspiracy theory books, and a certain New York real-estate developer at whom *Spy* magazine was always laughing.

(On YouTube, I once found an old Paramount theatrical newsreel from the late 1940s that looked back at the early 1930s and described the early Hitler as "someone we all thought was funny.")

If you like something with invisible "air quote" hand gestures, you're no better than the supposed "sheeple" you imagine to be its fans.

There was also a lot of lame parody (particularly in "comedy" movies) in the '80s-'90s. I don't mean sharp, socially-aware satire, but stuff that was darn-near indistinguishable from the "bad" media products it riffed on, that served up the same shticks only with "ironic" intent.

"Parody" and "satire" are often little more than lame excuses for what you really wanted to express anyway.

•

An even more dangerous form of "humor" is the bullying insult "joke."

Right-wing radio and cable-TV ranters, and online comment trolls, are full of it (as well as being more generally "full of it"). A few formerly-funny comedians (cf. Dennis Miller) have descended to it as their only remaining stock-in-trade.

It exists to bind its tellers and listeners in a shared, false sense of power and superiority over their supposed lessers (women, minorities, tree huggers, foreigners, "libtards," etc.).

And if you dare to tell the tellers of bullying insult "jokes" that they're not funny, they'll just turn their attacks on you, calling you part of the "politically-correct woke thought police" trying to "cancel" their daring voice of free speech.

If you're going to do something, mean it.

If you're going to like something, sincerely like it. You're not better than it; it's not better than you. It's just weird, and so are you, and so are all of us. Celebrate the cool and strange.

Avoid reading/watching/listening to any pop-culture product with an "ironic" smirk, just to silently laugh at its makers or at everyone else you imagine is reading/watching/listening to it.

We need more "metta" ("loving-kindness"), less "meta" (except for the definition of "meta" used in "metamodernism," as previously mentioned).

There are lots of expressions of "bad taste" that celebrate MISCosity. Among them:

- The flamboyant gay camp milieu. (A good resource about this scene and its roots is Philip Core's 1996 book *Camp: The Lie That Tells the Truth*, named from writer/artist/filmmaker Jean Cocteau's description of himself.)
- The joyously disgusting early films of John Waters, inspired by (and inspiring) gay camp.
- Glam rock, also largely inspired by gay camp.
- The overwrought excess of many Hollywood films (especially in the silent era), which helped inspire gay camp.
- The erotic and melodramatic excess of Russ Meyer's films (not officially inspired by gay camp).

'Camp' can be smug and tiresome, or it can be sincere and fabulous.

HEROES AND ZEROES

It is possible, as I've said, to sincerely and truly love weird sci-fi and horror movies, operatic heavy metal acts, even pro wrestling—with no need for distanced "irony," no need for air quotes. All it takes is connecting your senses and your funny bone to your heart.

Because it's exciting. Because it's fun. Because it brings you pleasure.

Art Chantry (whom I've mentioned previously) has noted that most of your '50s-'60s rebel movements (Beats, bikers, hot rodders, surfers, hippies, and early rock n' roll) had their roots in a generation of American men who came home from WWII to dull domestic lives in sterile suburbs, but who dreamed of a life with more adventure, more meaning—and, yes, more machismo, in which women ideally existed to have sex with men and then be tossed aside.

There are limits to "rebel bro" worship, and there are also limits to "bad boy" worship in films and TV shows about the Asshole Hero who "breaks all the rules" and always saves the day. (One TV critic noted that so many of those characters showed up in the 2000s because so many network and studio executives saw themselves that way.)

Early '70s "second wave" feminism was, in part, a reaction to male hippies and "radicals" who claimed to be "revolutionaries" but who often demanded that women take traditional, subservient roles.

THE MISCosity MANIFESTO

In the early 1990s, the major record labels tried to redefine "alternative" as a specific music genre with a specific range of styles, rather than what the term really meant—an attempt to produce and distribute music outside of the major-label system.

One of the things that the "alternative" or "indie" music scene/network wanted alternatives to was the trope of the Rock Star, the macho posturing baked into rock 'n roll, including punk rock. (As a *Harper's Magazine* critic once said about the Sex Pistols, "Rock 'n roll = boys doing bad things with guitars = maximum shock value.")

The town of my birth, Olympia WA, gave rise to a record label (still running today) called "Kill Rock Stars." It also generated the Riot Grrrls (radical/assertive bands and zine publishers intent on sparking a "revolution girl style") and Calvin Johnson (who recorded pensive teen love songs that he insisted were as "punk rock" as anything else).

•

Becoming a more MISCous person, becoming open to newer and more connections among people, requires you to dump some unproductive attitudes and behaviors.

So: no more excuses for brutal racism or sexism (not even, as we've said, when expressed in the form of "irony" or "jokes"). Yes, that includes white rappers whining about "why can't I say the N-word?"

Variant of an image originally designed by HE Creative in 2020.

PLEASURE PRINCIPLES

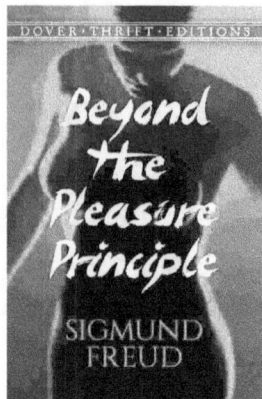

'Pleasure' as discussed by Sigmund Freud, Kate Soper, and adrienne maree brown.

Just as true "peace" means more than just the absence of armed conflict, true "pleasure" means more than just the absence of pain.

Pleasure as a deliberate life's pursuit has always been denounced in most industrialized nations (and especially in Britain and its ex-colonies).

Pleasure has often been disdained as:

- Romans enacting the brutal murders of slaves as an afternoon's entertainment,
- street drunks and syphilis-tainted streetwalkers,
- chronic gamblers ruining their families,
- lazy grasshoppers seeking a handout from industrious ants,
- the idle rich feeding parasitically on the workers,
- cheating spouses lured astray by conniving home wreckers,
- good-for-nothing dirty hippies,
- video game addicts who'll never move out of their parents' houses,
- TV-addled sheeple "amusing themselves to death" (as per Neil Postman), or
- degraded sluts, to be shamed for violating "proper" womanhood.

(Julie Peters in WANT: 8 Steps to Recovering Desire, Passion, and Pleasure After Sexual Assault): "Pleasure has always been policed, in some way or another, in cultures across the world. That's because pleasure is, in a way, a source of resistance.... It's a radical act of resistance against a history of suppression and pain. Taking pleasure, whether by enjoying great sex, going dancing, eating good food, or simply having a hot cup of tea on a cool day, is an act of self-determination and choice."

There are certain pleasures that can possibly (alcohol, overindulgence in certain foods, X-treme sports dares, promiscuous unprotected sex) or probably (meth, opioids, tobacco) harm or kill you.

And yes, you can take pleasure too far, to the point where it unbalances your life.

But you can do the same with work, or with social media. (For the moment, we'll set aside the question of whether compulsive screen-staring is really all that "pleasurable." To some, it is.)

•

Other art and aesthetic premises relate perfectly to MISCosity.

One is *Wabi-Sabi*, the Japanese worldview accepting transience and imperfection, championing a beauty of the impermanent, imperfect, and incomplete. Sometimes it's expressed as a broken tea bowl repaired in gold.

It ties in with a Buddhist premise of the "three marks of existence": impermanence, suffering, and emptiness.

As Robyn Griggs Lawrence puts it in *Natural Home* magazine (2001), Wabi-Sabi "...is everything that today's sleek, mass-produced, technology-saturated culture isn't. It's flea markets, not shopping malls; aged wood, not swank floor coverings; one single morning glory, not a dozen red roses. Wabi-sabi understands the tender, raw beauty of a gray December landscape and the aching elegance of an abandoned building or shed. It celebrates cracks and crevices and rot and all the other marks that time and weather and use leave behind. To discover wabi-sabi is to see the singular beauty in something that may first look decrepit and ugly."

THE IMPERFECT; THE EXOTIC

Martin Denny's 1957 LP Exotica was often played in basement tiki lounges across white America.

Thus, you can think of Wabi-Sabi as a way to not just "tolerate" diversity and imperfection, but to champion them.

In a sense, Wabi-Sabi is an opposite to exoticism, the depiction of foreign (or at least capital-O "Other") cultures as possessing some mystique or glamour.

And of course, exoticism is how almost the entire history of American popular music relates in some way to white guys copying Black sounds.

At its most benign, exoticism can be a way to bring new artistic concepts into Euro-American "mainstream" culture, as long as you know that's what you're doing. (Nobody who builds a tiki bar in their basement believes (I hope) that they're replicating real indigenous Hawai'ian sacred art.)

But at its most dangerous, exoticism can influence negative stereotypes—falsely typing young black men as violent, or Mexican Americans as lazy, or immigrants as somehow both taking citizens' jobs and living off of handouts, due to one-dimensional media characterizations.

It can get in the way of seeing other people as real people, as regular women and men and enbys, doing regular things, having regular dreams and desires.

Duke University Press blurb for a 2002 reprint of Victor Segalen's Essay on Exoticism: An Aesthetics of Diversity (1918): "The 'Other'—source of fear and fascination; emblem of difference demonized and romanticized."

Miscommunication and misunderstanding aren't just things the "old" cultural institutions spread, obviously.

They continue today in the online media, the "digital bride" that succeeded McLuhan's "Mechanical Bride."

The one medium to rule them all.

The successor or potential successor to the DVD, VCR, CD, still camera, movie/video camera, phonograph, newspaper, magazine, book, comic book, catalog, interoffice memo, mailbox, movie theater, radio, TV, teletype, fax, and really all forms of non-real-space media and the devices to record and play them.

(What online media hasn't yet replaced: the means to pay for the making of all this "content," and for creators to make a living creating. One reason why: most of the money from online ads is going not to creators but to "aggregators," the search engines and social media sites.)

The big social media sites aren't really about letting individuals express themselves, find like-minded souls, debate the issues of the day, or even share cute cat photos.

They exist to aggregate all these functions onto "massively multi-user" platforms, and to sell ads to more-and-more-precisely targeted sectors of that populace.

Media delivery, then and now.

Michael Harris's 2014 book *The End of Absence* notes how people born before, say, 1985 are the last people in the industrialized western world to have known a pre-Internet existence (let alone a pre-smartphone existence)—the last ones to have truly known the "daydreaming silences," the "burning solitudes" that so often get drowned out by the wired world's "continuous partial attention" and incessant multitasking.

Harris writes about how many online "user experiences" are carefully crafted to be as addictive as, say, casino gambling. Companies use relentless user testing to craft the most "sticky" experiences, giving off momentary dopamine pulses to the brain. News organizations strive to create irresistible "clickbait." Even "news items" based on provable facts are often still crafted to manipulate the emotions.

As Harris puts it, *"We push the technology down an evolutionary path that results in the most addictive possible outcome. Yet even as we do this, it doesn't feel as though we have any control. It feels, instead, like a destined outcome—a fate."*

Previous analog media were also carefully crafted, but with much less precision. To watch a film like David Cronenberg's 1983 *Videodrome*, which imagined analog broadcast TV and VHS cassettes as delivery systems for mind- and body-altering signals, is a wistful exercise in a strange form of nostalgia: *"Imagine! They thought such primitive technologies could transmit something that powerful. They didn't even have 5.1 surround sound yet, let alone 4K streaming!"*

'The continuing story of Another World'*

Nothing in human society is set in stone.

There is no divine right of kings, or of corporations.

The online realm was made by humans, and can be remade by humans. So can the offline realms, also known as "society."

There have always been people who worked to improve their communities and their societies.

And there have always been people who dreamed of even better social situations, better nations, better cultures, better worlds.

As a result of talking about a better world, people have made a lot of things happen.

We've now got indoor plumbing, electricity, wild and exotic foods, the lively arts, jet planes, satellite TV, pocket-size devices dispensing both literature and porn, and beer cans that show you when they're cold.

We've sent people to the moon and back.

We've gotten rid (mostly) of slavery and a bunch of horrid diseases (though others have shown up to take their place).

But we've still got war, poverty, exploitation, violence, and prejudice.

And the sphere on which we reside is ever-more hostile to the existence of our species.

So: We try, as we often have, to improve things on a "macro" scale.

Or at least we try to imagine how things could be improved.

*This title comes from the opening to a 1964-99 afternoon TV drama, created by the genre's founding mother Irna Phillips. Phillips originally explained that the title meant the internal 'world' of emotions and thought; similar to novelist George Eliot's 'invisible thoroughfares.'

MAKE YOUR OWN UTOPIA!

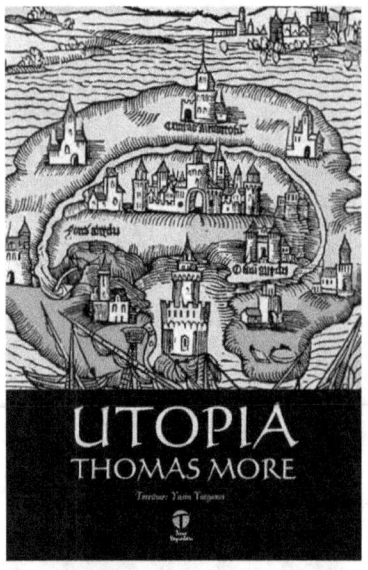

The term "utopia" literally means "nowhere." It was coined, in the novel of the same name, by Sir Thomas More. (He's otherwise best known for opposing King Henry VIII's ploy to kick the Catholic Church out of England, and getting beheaded for it.)

More's *Utopia* set the stage for so many to follow. As UK journalist Michael Caines put it, More envisioned: *"...a society founded on reason, organised rationally for the benefit of all. And the ultimate benefit of this rational hierarchy is pleasure–not just 'any kind of pleasure,' please, but only 'good and proper pleasure,' either for the body or the mind. You don't need to be a raging libertarian to realise that living in the Utopia of all Utopias, is strictly for those who are rational, egalitarian, and all but selfless."*

More's ideal nation has gender equality, free health care, communal eating, and no private property.

But it's also got slaves, bans premarital sex (under threat of enforced lifelong celibacy), and requires citizens to get an "internal passport" to travel to other sectors of the nation-state.

THE MISCosity MANIFESTO

Other literary and visual-media utopias:

- Edward Bellamy's *Looking Backward* (all "rational" like an American secular version of More, but with a "separate sphere" for women and no non-white people in sight).
- Ernest Callenbach's *Ecotopia* (Washington and Oregon as the remote provinces of a San Francisco city-state, with non-white people occasionally talked about but never seen).
- The 1930 film *Just Imagine* (your basic art-deco 250-story city of tomorrow, albeit with state-arranged marriages and people with numbers instead of names).
- The HG Wells-written 1936 film *Things To Come* (your basic post-conflict, underground-cities future, albeit having to emerge after decades of brutal global war).
- Even *Star Trek*, whose premise states that Earth-based humans have solved their own problems so they can go out and tackle the problems out in space or something like that. (Only to find out that every problem that can create a workable plot conflict has gone into space with them, or was already around when the Earth-based humans got there.)

Utopian fantasy is part of the larger multiverse of science fiction, fantasy, and horror. These genres can (and sometimes do) open the mind and heart to new possibilities.

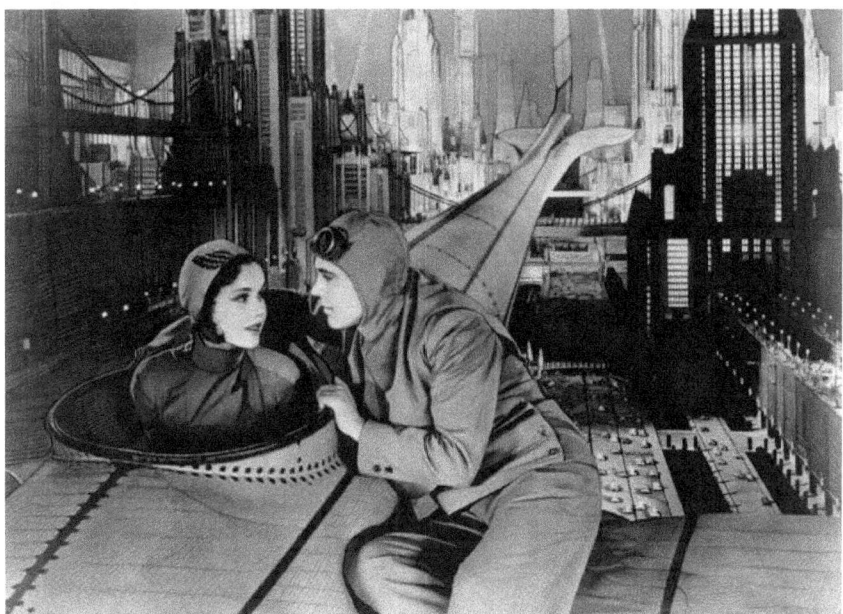

Quasi-forbidden romance amid the 1930s futurism of Just Imagine.

FUTURES PAST 112

So it's sad to see these genres often retreat into tired reactionary worldviews; leading to the virulent sexism of Gamergate, the selfish Ayn Rand-ism of much of Silicon Valley, and also to the "Darth Vader admiration" aspect of the "alt-right." None of this is new.

SF author Michael Moorcock's 1977 essay "Starship Stormtroopers" criticized "the saturation of Fascistic and authoritarian themes and messages" in science fiction:

"Utopian fiction has been predominantly reactionary in one form or another (as well as being predominantly dull) since it began. Most of it warns the world of 'decadence' in its contemporaries and the alternatives are usually authoritarian and sweeping—not to say simple-minded...."

"There is Lovecraft, the misogynistic racist; there is Heinlein, the authoritarian militarist; there is Ayn Rand, the rabid opponent of trade unionism and the left, who, like many a reactionary before her, sees the problems of the world as a failure by capitalists to assume the responsibilities of 'good leadership'; there is Tolkien and that group of middle-class Christian fantasists who constantly sing the praises of bourgeois virtues and whose villains are thinly disguised working class agitators—fear of the Mob permeates their rural romances. To all these and more the working class is a mindless beast which must be controlled or it will savage the world (i.e. bourgeois security)— the answer is always leadership, 'decency', paternalism (Heinlein is particularly strong on this), Christian values..."

But the realms of fantasy can also open minds.

They can symbolically express new, different ways of looking at the allegedly "real" world.

And they can explore other worlds—worlds that could exist, or that couldn't exist but can show us how to live in ours.

An example of fantasy as symbol of "reality": poet/painter William Blake (1757-1827) and his elaborate "invented mythology," full of *"original concepts, gods, places, and terms"* (as described by Maggie McNeill). Among his concepts were a hierarchy of four "states of being" according to the number of "eyes" one has open:

Ulro, the lowest state, *"is the internal condition of blackness, opacity, and darkness which occurs when the Divine Vision is lost."* (Ellie Clayton) *"People who exist this way can be visualized as going through the world with one eye closed, seeing everything flat and without proper perspective."* (McNeill)

Generation is *"dominated by the genitals and can be imagined as seeing with both eyes."* (McNeill) In this state of mind, *"there's more room for pondering the creation of life on a biological scale."* (Susanna Andrews)

Beulah, *"a pleasant lovely Shadow/ Where no dispute can come"* (Blake), occurs *"when the individual is open to the spiritual or imaginative dimension"* (McNeill). It's *"the world of the passive emotions—quiet, tender, given over to outward emotions and dreamy institutions."* (Milton O. Percival); and is *"characterized by 'threefold vision,' which one might think of as the 'third eye' of mysticism, the 'altered consciousness' experienced by psychedelic drug users, an ecstatic religious state or even a transcendent erotic experience"* (McNeill).

At the top: *Eternity*, also known as *Eden*, with *"fourfold vision"*: *"a condition of total bliss which few humans can reach, and even then only for very short periods of time while existing in this plane"* (McNeill).

William Blake, Our Time Is Fix'd, 1743.

OTHER WORLDS, OTHER VISIONS

H.P. Lovecraft's horror mythos is innately tied in with his virulent racism, something some of his modern-day fans prefer not to think about. In Lovecraft the horror always comes from a monster that isn't "alien" (from another planet) but is definitely of "The Other," as are the non-white people who are often depicted as the monster's cult followers, equally as deserving of slaughter as the monster itself.

A few other, perhaps more encouraging, examples of the possibilities of other worlds:

- Ursula K. Le Guin's various women-run worlds, some more "utopian" than others. (i.e., no singular collective gender hive mind.)
- Octavia Butler's *Patternist* series: A secret history from ancient Egypt into the future, with race/gender conflicts and other power plays continuing from past to future.
- Marge Piercy's *Woman on the Edge of Time*: Everybody lives essentially apart; full gender equality; no "him" or "her" pronouns.
- "Hope punk" fiction and the attempt to revive, if not Utopias, at least the idea that better societies could arise from the current miasma of despair.

Art installation by Nathan Coley (based on a Talking Heads song lyric) in Foklestone UK, 2008.

But back to fantasized utopias. Most of them have three big problems:

- A world where all conflict is removed is a world without (as we've seen) a basic element of a traditional story. The plots in utopian fiction usually consist of outside threats to the inside perfect place, or simple travelogues through the perfect place, or historic (or future-historic) accounts of how the perfect place comes into being.

- Most of these ideal-world concepts don't include a practical "road map" for how to get there. Some present a perfect society that's simply always been around. Some (including More's original *Utopia*) require a "benevolent dictator" or "philosopher king" to impose an ideal order onto society, even if this grand designer somehow disappears from the picture afterwards. Others require a "war to end all wars" somehow bringing about world peace.

- But the biggest problem with almost all fantasy utopias (and many attempts at real-world utopias) is that they're built around the way-too-simple premise that "the world would be perfect if everybody was Just Like Me."

UTOPIA AND UNIFORMITY 116

Poster art for Being John Malkovich *(1999).*

Most fantasy utopias (and most attempted real-world utopias) are extreme monocultures. They've got only one type of people, with a very narrow range of tastes and ideas.

Thus, you have perfect futures where everybody's a free-marketer, or a socialist worker, or a technocrat, or a Catholic, or a vegan, or a gun-toting survivalist.

Heck, some utopian fantasies only have one gender (or only one predominant gender). There's either men running everything (still) with women in the background, or there's women running everything with men as submissives (or nonexistent).

If you can't even imagine a future where cis-females and cis-males of the same ethnicity and culture can co-exist as equals, how can you imagine a future where different ethnicities and cultures do likewise?

This affects visions of the "real" world and what it should be or become.

One example: the "techno utopians," about whom we'll talk in a few pages.

Dystopia is the opposite of utopia.

Instead of a glorious future, the many flavors of dystopia feature characters fighting for survival (and not always making it) in worlds gone terribly, horribly wrong.

Many of those worlds are under the thumb of One Big Menace: zombies, conquerors from space, invaders from foreign lands, sexist religious cults, corporate oligarchies, quasi-Stalinist or quasi-Hitlerist dictators. Often, the One Big Menace is a simple trend from the author's present time taken to its extreme (i.e., just as monocultural as most utopian fantasies).

Dystopias are also arguably the most popular science fiction/fantasy tropes these days.

It's easy to see why.

Many people see a rising dystopia all around them, between a planet slowly going kablooey, economic stagnation for non-zillionaires, the personal brutalities of social media, and in politics, well....

In that context, stories about individuals and small groups learning to somehow survive, and to win at least small victories over the zombies/overlords/invaders/sexists/racists/dictators, are stories of hope.

ONE PERSON'S HEAVEN, ANOTHER PERSON'S HELL 118

But, just as most "heroic" stories are structured to showcase a specific type of hero, survival fiction is typically structured around a specific view of the "real" world.

Zombie dystopias, as an example, are often constructed to favor a survivalist-militia worldview: the outside world is evil, strangers are presumed to be hostile sub-humans, don't trust outsiders, always be armed and ready to kill.

There's also the dystopia trope of a utopia for a few surrounded by hell for the many, or a utopia for only for a limited time span. (Some examples: E.M. Forster's 1909 story *The Machine Stops*, the 1976 film *Logan's Run*, Spielberg's early TV movie *LA 2017*, and the real-world attempts to create "billionaires' bunkers.")

But surviving under the world's current circumstances isn't enough.

We must change those circumstances (threatened ecosystems, massive economic inequality, brutal authoritarian regimes, hate and bigotry everywhere, etc.)

Not in some fantasized future, not with fanciful tech, but in the here and now with what we've got.

We not only must, we can.

THE MISCosity MANIFESTO

There have been countless visions of a better world (in the "real" world, as opposed to fiction) over the centuries.

There were the Paris Commune, the Israeli Kibbutz movement, and pre-Leninist visions of commune-ism.

There were North American millennial and communitarian movements. The Shakers, the Roycrofters, etc. etc. Most didn't last, or they morphed into something else, as we mentioned previously.

Some other better-world formulae:

- Technocracy, a vision of a world run by a "rational" state.
- The "black cat" cooperative movement, a vision of a world run by radical small enterprises working together. A small chain of lumber yards in the Northwest was one of its legacies.
- The International Workers of the World (the most radical labor movement the US ever had), and its vision of a world run by "one big union of all the workers."
- The Leninist and/or Trotskyite visions of an industrial but egalitarian society, that somehow would emerge from a rigidly hierarchical, militaristic regime.
- Ayn Rand's equally impractical notion of a free-market utopia in which everybody's narrow self-interest would somehow even out into shining greatness.
- Charles Fourier's notion of anarchy with gender equality as well as "free love."

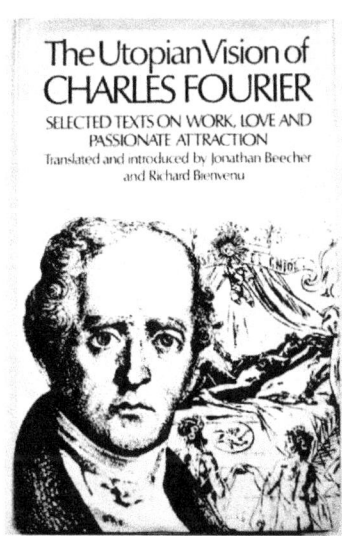

Concept art for 'Blueseed,' a Peter Thiel-backed 2013 idea of a floating city-state in international waters where rich techies would always have their way.

- Murray Bookchin's notion of a "post-scarcity anarchism."
- The idea, promoted most recently by tech billionaires, of a guaranteed annual income. (The techies like it because they'd feel less guilty about replacing most human jobs with robots and other automation.)
- The notion, mostly developed in San Francisco, of a new (mostly white, mostly male, all wealthy) elite bringing "disruptive technologies" to wipe away the detritus of the old order (such as labor rights). The resulting tech-bro heaven/hell that took over that and other cities was not a break from that city's bohemian hedonistic tradition but one outgrowth from it that mutated and metastasized. (About the only aspects of the tech-bro "utopias" that haven't come true for evil yet: 1) built-from-scratch "new cities" or even new nation-states (completely corporate-libertarian of course; though now many of these tycoons are asserting big influence in the US's ruling regime), and 2) the more advanced versions of "teledildonics," fantasies about robotic masturbation toys.)

World building includes not only utopias/dystopias, but conceptions about the world we live in now, about our world's past, and about other fictional societies (on this and on other spheres).

The worlds we co-build are all around us. Author Jane Jacobs wrote in 1961 in praise of "the ballet of the street" and the value of the civic center or *agora*:

"It is a complex order. Its essence is intricacy of sidewalk use, bringing with it a constant succession of eyes. This order is all composed of movement and change, and although it is life, not art, we may fancifully call it the art form of the city and liken it to the dance."

These phenomena were specifically lobbied against by conservative planners even before the dawn of suburbia, because lively streets are where people of different cultures and castes commingle, spreading ideas and zeitgeists, mixing n' matching cultural influences.

•

A true "movement," like any transportation (moving) event, requires knowing three things as best as you can know them:

- Where you are,
- Where you want to be, and
- How you plan to get there.

And then: Really DOING what it takes to get there.

WHAT'S YOUR 'PHASE 2'?

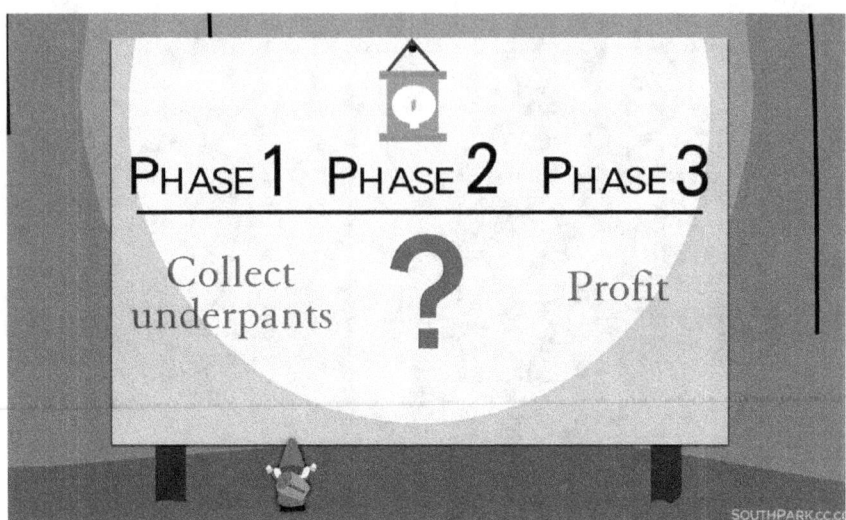

Left wingers love to delineate the present ordeal in endless (depressing) detail, and sometimes to rhapsodize about the glory days of a potential future. But in between those time frames, they're often like the gnomes in a *South Park* episode who plan to profit from stealing underpants but just don't know how that would work.

Or they resort to the same old tactics that haven't accomplished much except make them feel righteous. Marches, petitions, destructive "direct actions," "movements" that devolve into personality cults, sloganeering.sloganeering.sloganeering, internecine verbal warfare against those who almost agree with you but not completely.

•

Then there's the right-wing, authoritarian/fundamentalist ideology, which has gotten so "purified" as to become brittle and breakable.

At the time of this writing, that ideology has become further bent into a personality cult around a small group of nakedly corrupt, bigoted, and brutal manipulators with some "useful idiot" front people. You can expect the ideology to stick around even after its current cult leaders have left the public stage.

It's not new, and it's not an anomaly. It's something that's been a part of the US since the Indian wars, slavery, the century of Jim Crow laws that followed slavery, overseas wars of colonial conquest, CIA-backed foreign coups and dictatorships, and churches that promoted "Christian" excuses for all of the above and more.

The ideology of conquest, subjugation, and supposed moral superiority is pretty much baked into our nation's (and many other nations') standard operating procedure.

You may have heard of the concept of "American exceptionalism," the notion that the US is somehow immune to the rest of humanity's social and political shticks, and that Americans are a higher species than rest-of-the-worlders (despite most of us having non-Indigenous ancestry).

There's also the notion that oneself, and those in one's own bubble subculture, are a higher species than ordinary mainstream Americans.

You can find the latter notion in an aspect of the hippie/boomer ideology that came to inspire the early tech bros—the concept that an insider elite was innately superior to the "hick" masses (and even more so over non-white and non-male people); leading "logically" to the notion that only the insiders' wants or needs were worth considering. ("So what if all the laundromats in town are getting evicted? Who needs laundromats when we have dry-cleaning delivery dot-coms?")

(Ijeoma Oluo to Greg Epstein, TechCrunch.com): "One thing tech fundamentally has in common with many religions, at least in America, is that it is a white man's version of Utopia. And tech especially has this cult-like adherence to a white man's vision of a Utopia that fundamentally disempowers and endangers women and people of color."

But what to do about it?

WHAT'S 'WINNING' ANYWAY?

A modest proposal (really, it is quite modest indeed) for what to do:

- No purist ideology of any sort.
- No false notion of exceptionalism or immunity from human imperfections.
- No false notion of personal superiority—and all such notions are false.
- And, as we've said: No master race, no master gender, no master clique, no master caste, no master nation, no master food regimen, no master music genre, and especially no masters.

Instead:

- A world where "weirdness" is not something to be crushed but to be celebrated.
- A world where all the nationalities, all the ethnicities, all the cultures are cherished, where everybody gets along as best as they can.
- A messy world.
- A multiplicious world.
- A MISCous world.
- Not a world where all the problems are solved forever (which could never happen anyway).
- But a world with the greatest ability to handle what problems come along, because it has the widest possible range of approaches and ideas available.

THE MISCosity MANIFESTO

Mixing it up (in the right proportions): Good for recipes, good for societies, good for economies.

Also:

- A mixed (or MISC) economy and socio-political system.
- The politics of Whatever Works. Using the business, government, and nonprofit sectors for whichever things they're good at. Creating new models for whatever new challenges arise.
- Choosing what to do on the basis of what needs doing; not necessarily what makes the most money for influential interests or political donors, or what makes the already powerful more powerful.
- Junking hip cynicism, the rule of gold, and outrage-porn media.
- Empowering people of color, immigrants, women, queers, trans-folk, etc., not as damsels or waifs in need of rescue by some (usually white, usually male) hero, but as individuals, families, and "tribes" who can build their own futures.

(Slogan of autistic self-advocates, among others: "Nothing about us without us.")

We don't need (at least not in this country, at least not yet) to violently overthrow anything. Those kinds of "revolutions" almost always end in dictatorships or reigns of terror, for very predictable reasons.

Besides, not everything billed as "revolutionary" is.

Certainly not the dot-com era hype, recently dusted off for the AI era, about "a revolution in business."

What we may need instead is a "revolution" *away from* business, or rather away from the notion that "the business of America is business" (a phrase attributed alternately to President Calvin Coolidge and to General Motors head Alfred Sloan).

Entrepreneur/activist Nick Hanauer, in a 2018 speech at MIT, said we need to get rid of the notion of "Homo Economicus," the idea that people are *"perfectly selfish, perfectly rational, and relentlessly self-maximizing."* Instead: *"Homo sapiens have evolved to be other-regarding, reciprocal, heuristic, and intuitive moral creatures…. Pro-sociality is our economic super power."*

The true business of any nation, any people, is to tend to its people and to its land. Not to serve a king (or guru or teacher), not to deliver value for shareholders (or political campaign donors), not to be rich and famous, not to "die with the most toys," not to land the most bedmates, not to achieve the perfect look or the highest social status.

Conservative columnist George F. Will: "The business of America is not business. Neither is it war. The business of America is justice and securing the blessings of liberty."

We don't need to tear the fabric of society apart. Big business already did it. We need to sew it back together.

So: A movement, as big as the planet and as small as your own personal circles.

A movement to get things done. To make real progress for the most people.

(adrienne maree brown, Emergent Strategy):"Change is definitely going to happen, no matter what we plan or expect or hope for or set in place. We will adapt to that change, or we will become irrelevant."

Make sure your "movement" is run by the same principles on which you want the world to be run. Otherwise, "six months from now you'll be stealing Erno's nose" (a line in *Sleeper*, a film by the now-disgraced Woody Allen).

Avoid relying on "charismatic" leaders, or on prioritizing the organization above getting real shit done. (Many of the "Occupy ____" protests of 2011-12 eventually devolved from being about "the 99 percent" to just being about defending the protest camps themselves.)

The Colonial Flag
THE COLONIAL LIFE INSURANCE COMPANY OF AMERICA, JERSEY CITY, N.J.

THE DANCE OF CHANGE

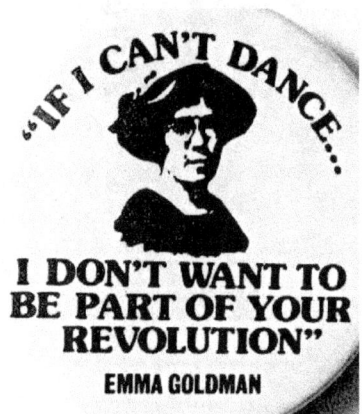

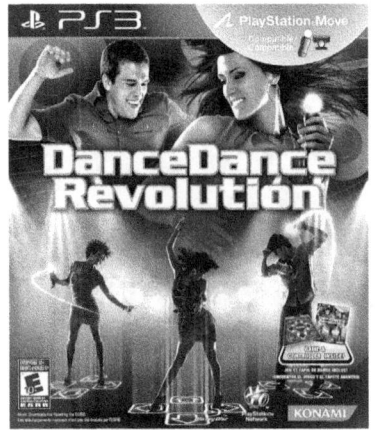

And don't get in the trap, as many of my boomer elders did, of trying to do everything just like it was done in "the sixties" (or rather, in a specific piece of "the sixties").

A subset of original hippiedom was about pursuing hedonist leisure (the old "sex n' drugs n' rock n' roll") marketed as something "revolutionary," while real social and political change was being worked for, with costs and consequences, by others.

A study of what really happened in "the sixties" would mainly focus on the likes of MLK, Cesar Chavez, the Greensboro Woolworth sit-in, the Civil Rights Act, the "Long Hot Summer" race riots, the Pill, the feminist explosion, the Stonewall riots, etc., and on the counter-revolutions of George Wallace and Richard Nixon; and not solely on white affluent college kids sowing their wild oats.

Hedonism, after all, has been practiced among the affluent classes for centuries all over the world, without upending said classes' privileges.

But the hippies had one vital and true idea: Politics is a subset of culture, not the other way around. Creating a new politics is dependent on creating a new culture.

There are no ideological short cuts to amending the established world views of the millions, one set of ears, one set of eyes, one set of (possibly dancing) feet at a time.

"Only love will save the world." (A line in the last scene of the 2017 Wonder Woman *movie, and in the final opening theme of the Irna Phillips-created* Guiding Light.*)*

THE MISCosity MANIFESTO

Becoming a more MISCous person.

Changing the world is work. Anything that's really valuable is.

But it can be SO worth it.

One way to start the process:

- Imagine an ideal future human society, or at least a better one. One that's different from most imagined utopias: A place where everyone (not just people similar to yourself) takes care and is taken care of.
- Then: Imagine how someone such as you would live in such a place; what you'd become.
- Then: Start to become that person now.

I've put this part between the part about collective imaginations and a part about cooperative striving, because I don't want you to think of yourself above all.

This isn't a "self-improvement" routine.

Nor is it a "self-deprecation" routine.

It's not even a "self-actualization" routine.

It's a "self-integration" routine.

It's a way to welcome and accept all the disparate parts of your "self," at the same time as you welcome and accept all the disparate parts of the society, and the world, surrounding you.

It's becoming what you really already are—a strange, diverse piece of a strange, diverse world.

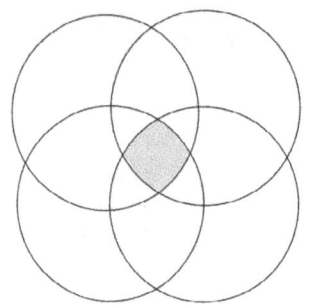

Remember:

- Everybody's weird (including you).
- Nobody's superior (not even you).
- You're not the biggest or best thing in the world; and neither is your "tribe," your "nation," or even your species or your planet.

Alan Watts, whom we've mentioned a few times already, wrote about the fiction of the separate "self," that really we're all part of the one being that is Life on Earth, which is part of the one being that is, well, everything.

(Mike Elliott (often misattributed to Flannery O'Connor)): "You shall know the truth, and the truth shall make you odd."

•

What are you *really*?

A human "being" or a human "doing" (as per Eckhart Tolle, who prefers the former)?

A creature driven by *"Homo faber"* (a Marxist notion that we are primarily working beings who create themselves through their labor); or by *"Eros"* (passion, play, desire; as posited by Herbert Marcuse)?

•

What's the purpose of your life? Have you ever asked yourself?

Ikigai (a Japanese term for one's life purpose or destiny) has been interpreted as a four-part Venn Diagram intersecting your *passion* (what you love), your *mission* (what the world needs), your *vocation* (what you are good at), and your *profession* (what you can get paid for).

Andrew Harvey writes in *The Hope: A Guide to Sacred Activism* that we should be "following our heartbreak" (as opposed to Joseph Campbell's "follow your bliss").

But still, discerning what you love, *"what makes you come alive"* (Howard W. Thurman), is a good place to start.

•

Some hints about your, my, and our purpose(s) in life:

- It's not about self-help (only).
- It's not about superficial consumer "happiness."
- It's not about acquiring stuff, or status, or a spouse/family/booty call.
- It's not about conquering, getting, or "winning."
- It's not about becoming what your family/church/peer group wants you to become.
- It's not about either conforming to or rebelling against any notion of a "mainstream."
- It's not even about "peace of mind."

It's about being a proud, loving, idiosyncratic weirdo among a species full of idiosyncratic weirdos.

It's about getting along with all these other individuals, while celebrating both your individuality and theirs.

And it's about making things better–for yourself, your loved ones, and your extended family (i.e. everybody).

HOPE OR NOPE?

And:

It's about being aware of the chaos, the intricacy, the complexity of life, without falling into a false simplification or a false sense of separateness/superiority.

There is no instant karma, no sudden awakening.

Except to *really see*.

And when you *really see*, everything changes.

•

This is often, traditionally, called "enlightenment."

But it's not the "blinding light" that renders you incapable of perceiving the darkness.

It's the mental/spiritual/cosmic "light" that reveals the darkness in all its tender detail.

St. Paul's reference to "the peace of God, that passes [surpasses] all understanding" correctly implies that total "understanding" is impossible.

And that's perfectly OK!

You don't have to understand everything.

You don't have to know everything.

And you sure don't have to imagine (falsely) that you know everything (which you can't).

You don't need a full hi-res satellite-view image to know where you're going. A simple road map works just as well.

Or just a flashlight in front of your feet.

The light, just enough light, to keep your mind and your self forging ahead (or on a particularly interesting digression): that's hope.

And it's something we all need.

A good working definition of hope could be a deep, active desire (not just an abstract wish) for a better life and a better world.

The kind of eager desire that makes you work, as best you can, to make it come true.

The kind that keeps you going, in spite of everything.

(Tagline for the film The Shawshank Redemption): "Fear can hold you prisoner. Hope can set you free."

(Emily Dickinson): "Hope is the thing with feathers that perches in the soul."

Hope is something different from the relentless "positivity" promoted in fashion media, and in books and training programs meant to give you a sales-hustler mentality.

No, everybody's not meant to have a sales-hustler mentality. Indeed, it's probably not a healthy way to live.

Og Mandino's book The Greatest Salesman in the World imagines Jesus as the ultimate sales-networker dude. As extreme interpretations of Jesus go (and there are many), it's relatively benign but still doesn't get the point about the guy who forced the money-changers out of the Temple.

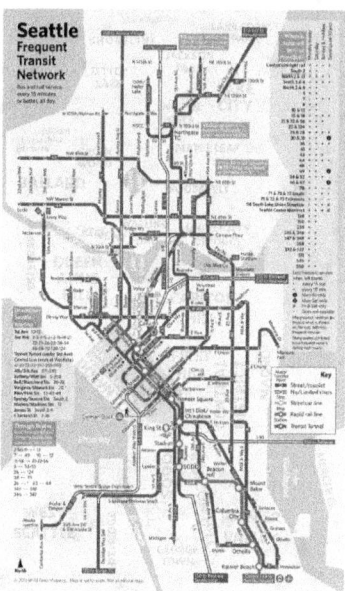

By Seattle Transit Blog.

'SANE INSANITY'

Late 20th century updates of the comedy and tragedy faces, of a sort.

And hope is also something different from some definitions of "happiness," as a mindless state of constant giddiness or an acceptance of things in the world that shouldn't be accepted.

Who really needs that? There's no *yang* without *yin* and vice versa. No "comedy" without "tragedy."

(In the 1970s, a neighborhood movie theater in my city switched from "art" (i.e. foreign) films to porn. It changed its sign, which had displayed the traditional theatrical symbols of the comedy and tragedy masks, to one where both faces were smiling. An unwitting symbol of that genre's unrealistic insistence on "pleasure" without "pain.")

Another definition of hope is wishing + taking action.

Action to make a better situation, a better world, for you, your loved ones, your "tribe," and the larger world.

Even when the situation, the "game," isn't set up in your favor.

I.e., in "real" life, not a fictional setup designed to showcase a hero's "superior" will and determination.

•

Most fictional heroes, of the "action" or "super" or other types, always win ONLY in fictional constructs set up to make/let them win. Yes, even when the author sets up a bunch of obstacles that our particular hero is uniquely able to overcome.

THE MISCosity MANIFESTO

Many "political" novels and utopian premises also rely on carefully constructed situations devised to generate the desired "heroic victory" ending. Ayn Rand's "heroes," like her political/economic systems, just wouldn't make it in anything approaching the "real" world.

These "real"-world limits also apply to the "bad boy rebel" and "asshole winner" tropes. Inconsiderate jerks (men who treat women as disposable sex toys; cops who "break all the rules"; bosses who bully and abuse their workers): not real "winners," not role models to be admired or emulated.

Indeed, what's "winning" mean in those protagonists' contexts?

Usually, it really means feeling superior.

Which nobody really is, as we keep saying.

Since no one is "normal," no one is, by any potential standard definition, "sane."

The School of Life, a website co-run by Alain de Botton, describes "sane insanity," instead of "sanity," as a good personal goal: *"The sane insane differ from the simply insane by virtue of the honest and accurate grasp they have on what is not entirely right with them."*

(Attributed to Leo Buscaglia): *"In a crazy world, it's only your insanity that will keep you sane."*

In the case of stressing out over uncertainty (one of many causes or at least triggers of mental anguish), about realizing what you don't know; and about realizing that you don't know.

And that not knowing is not only inevitable, but it's OK.

'You can't fool me! There ain't no sanity clause.' (A Night at the Opera, 1935)

COOKING WITH 'GAS'

You don't have to let not-knowing trigger feelings of anxiety. And if those feelings show up anyway, you can step back into "observing" mode and understand.

Yes, you don't know whether you'll get that job/your crush will love you back/your candidate will win the election/your team will win the big game/that college will take you in/a loved one will or won't recover from a health scare/the climate can survive/humanity can survive.

And yes, your life, and the lives of others, will be inexorably changed by the outcome of any or all of these.

And the not-knowing stresses you like all get-out.

And that's how it is. It just is.

Some definitions of "insanity," even definitions promoted over the years by governments and the medical establishment, are dangerously close to merely "atypical." Lesbians and gay men were routinely locked up as supposedly insane in many places (or simply jailed or sent to detention facilities in other places).

"Insanity" can also be used as a fear tactic by domestic abusers, such as the cruel husband in the play and film *Gaslight*. To this day, "gaslighting" is a term for telling someone that they're not really seeing/hearing/experiencing, well, what they're really seeing/hearing/experiencing. ("What do you believe, me or your own eyes?")

Still, there are particular mental manifestations/states that aren't good for you and/or those around you.

Stepping back in your head and knowing what's going on in your head is a good immediate response, but many of us need longer-range solutions.

There are many books on how to find which solutions work for you (which could involve various combos of therapy, medication, lifestyle changes, and mental discipline). My friend Ellen Forney's books *Marbles* and *Rock Steady* are based on her own bipolar life, but also have lessons and tools for folks with many other conditions, such as depression, anxiety, and ADHD (which isn't just for kids, you know).

(1970s bumper sticker: "Just because you're paranoid, it doesn't mean they're not out to get you.")

(Comedian Aparna Nancherla on the COVID-19 crisis and people with chronic anxiety):"This is our Olympics."

•

Nearly every fundamentalist religion/philosophy/clique/conspiracy theory/cult offers freedom from uncertainty. I don't.

Early tech blogger Dave Winer talked about computer/tech people and outfits (notably Microsoft) deliberately spreading "FUD" (fear, uncertainty, doubt) about other outfits' technologies and products.

You can and should get over the fear part as much as you can.

But uncertainty and doubt: they are, have always been, and always will be.

In MISCosity, doubt and ambiguity are not dragons to be slain but "givens" to live beside and within, parts of the natural environment of the mind. One can no more banish doubt and ambiguity from one's life than one can banish oxygen from one's life (and expect to remain living).

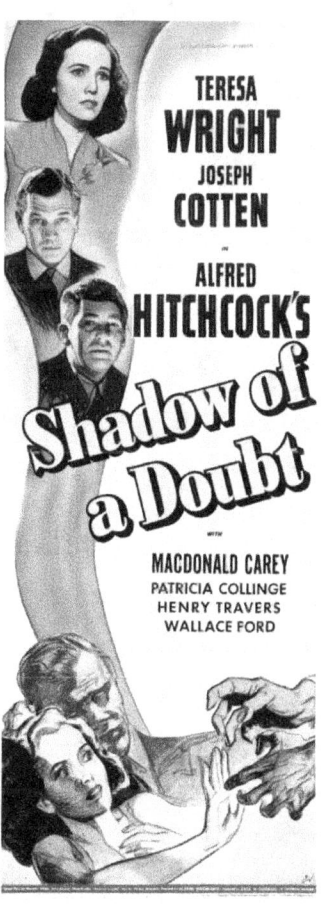

Knowing that you can't ever know everything, and accepting it (grudgingly if need be), is infinitely more realistic than buying into one false certainty or another, no matter which one it is.

•

In decreasing order of value:
- *Wisdom.*
- *Insight.*
- *Intelligence.*
- *Knowledge.*
- *Information.*
- *Data.*

•

Hipster "irony," that detached and "above it all" attitude toward media, culture, and even life itself, has devolved into just one more defense against honestly facing your own emotions, your own consciousness.

It's often also just a lame excuse for doing bad or stupid things.

(David Foster Wallace, in an NPR interview):"Irony and sarcasm and all that stuff are fantastic for exploding hypocrisy and exposing what's wrong in extant values. As far as I can see, they're notably less good at erecting replacement values or coming any closer to the truth. And the thing about it is they're a terrific tool and they were used really well. We're just still using it, it seems to me, as a culture, 35, 40 years after it really had some use. And the thing about it is they're a terrific tool and they were used really well. We're just still using it, it seems to me, as a culture, 35, 40 years after it really had some use."

When you truly know how little you know, how little you can ever know, it can help you to "quiet your ego." That's something Scott Barry Kaufman suggested as a "pressing need" in order to "strengthen your best self" in a 2018 *Scientific American* piece:

"The goal of the quiet ego approach is to arrive at a less defensive, and more integrative stance toward the self and others, not lose your sense of self or deny your need for the esteem from others. You can very much cultivate an authentic identity that incorporates others without losing the self, or feeling the need for narcissistic displays of winning. A quiet ego is an indication of a healthy self-esteem, one that acknowledges one's own limitations, doesn't need to constantly resort to defensiveness whenever the ego is threatened, and yet has a firm sense of self-worth and competence."

London ad man Paul Arden presents a counter-argument in his book *Whatever You Think, Think the Opposite*: Great people have great egos; maybe that's what makes them great. But Arden's definition of "ego" is *"individual creativity without censor filters,"* rather than pompous, selfish arrogance.

•

Healing after a moment or a lifetime of abuse or oppression (sexual, physical, emotional, social, racial, and/or political) requires learning, again or for the first time, about the complexities in life, in other people, and in oneself. Otherwise, one is stuck in the mental loop of eternal outrage, in the artificially narrow worldview of "abuser, victim, avenger" (another variation of the so-called "Hegelian dialectic").

I'm not telling you your abuse (of whatever sort or sorts) never happened, or asking you to behave as if it never happened. It was/is almost certainly all too real, and it really damaged your mind and spirit and (in some cases) your body.

Rather, I'm asking you to do what you can to heal yourself from those wounds. Not to forget what happened to you, but also not to stay hindered by it.

I'd say likewise for those who've been abusing themselves (emotionally and/or chemically), probably as a reaction to and/or continuation of abuse done by others.

There are hundreds of books about emotionally and mentally healing yourself. My late mother had her favorites. You can try one, then another. Eventually, if you develop the right kind of self-awareness, you can determine what works for you, then keep working at it.

THE MISCosity MANIFESTO

The parts of common self-help prescriptions that I do believe in:

- Generosity, gratitude, and healthy humility are some of the things to grab on to. Then you might have a crack at a decent life.
- Being impeccable with your word (as per Don Miguel Ruiz's *The Four Agreements*). That means more than merely not lying. To me, it also means that if you say something, mean it. Don't tell bigoted insults, then claim they were just "jokes."
- Doing what you set out to do. (Or in the words of Larry the Cable Guy, "Git 'er done.")
- Treating yourself with dignity and respect, but not with delusions of superiority.
- (Uncommon) common sense.
- The premise of constant renewal. The world is a circle....
- Never proclaiming yourself to be "done," or "perfected." Nobody ever is.

•

Becoming a better person does not equal becoming an abusive person yourself.

No matter how much certain elements in society praise, as we've mentioned, "the asshole who gets things done," or "the prick who turns out to be always right," or "the disruptor."

The problem with creeps isn't just that they're creeps. It's also that they think it's "cool" to be creeps.

Spoiler alert: It isn't cool to be a creep, and it never was.

No matter what certain creeps in commercial media, social media, and high corporate and political positions may claim.

STAYING FLUID 142

The "viscosity" part of MISCosity has to do with being solid yet fluid in your mind and spirit, flowing through a world more complex than any of us can ever understand.

When I thought of the premise, I didn't know that *"fluid intelligence"* was already a long-standing concept.

It was coined by psychologist Raymond Cattell in 1963, and further developed by his onetime student John L. Horn.

The term has a counterpart, *"crystallized intelligence."*

To be over-simplistic (as everything in this book has been), the basic idea is that "fluid intelligence" is formless, and can "flow into" a wide variety of activities and disciplines; while the "crystallized" mind has its ways of thinking set in proverbial stone, and can only add new information and viewpoints as long as they build upon a set "foundation."

Human individuals are capable of both "fluid" and "crystallized" senses of learning and knowing.

But: *"Fluid intelligence peaks at around age 20 and then gradually declines."* (Wikipedia)

The trick, then, is to remain fully capable of "fluid thinking" well into adulthood.

Christopher Bergland, at *Psychology Today* in 2013, defined fluid intelligence as: *"...The capacity to think logically and solve problems in novel situations, independent of acquired knowledge. Fluid intelligence involves the ability to identify patterns and relationships that underpin novel problems and to extrapolate these findings using logic. On the other hand, crystallized intelligence is the ability to utilize information, skills, knowledge, and experience in a way that could be measured on a standardized test."*

My own definition of "fluid" thinking: to use logic and intuition interdependently, to assess new situations, to devise new solutions (or apply old solutions in new ways), to respond to new and old problems (and, in a sense, they're all really "old problems"). To keep one's mind not only open to new ideas but to new ways of processing those ideas. To never stop thinking or imagining. To never stop truly hearing, truly seeing.

It's also similar to an idea promoted by post-WWII French intellectuals Claude Levi-Strauss and Jacques Derrida, encouraging people to think and act like *"bricoleurs"* (DIY artists and craftspeople, assembling things from whatever materials happen to be around) instead of like "engineers" (strictly proceeding according to pre-established rules).

Claude Levi-Strauss (1908-2009) made sociocultural theory, not jeans.

A 1957 essay by Julian Huxley (brother of *Brave New World* novelist Aldous Huxley) popularized *transhumanism*, the concept of "refining and improving the human species" (Britannica.com).

While earlier "eugenics" advocates (including the Nazis) talked of selectively breeding supposedly "superior" people and even killing the supposedly "inferior," transhumanists generally prefer to claim the technologies they study (ranging from genetic engineering to "brain chips") could benefit the species as a whole, even as they lead toward a potential new ("posthuman") species.

Or alternately, our digital creations could simply surpass us and take us over.

Many imagined futures, at least since Karel Čapek's 1920 play *R.U.R.*, have depicted computers, androids, and robots as full characters (as good, evil, and everything in between).

My earliest memory of the initials "A.I." was as the title of one of Steven Spielberg's lesser movies (about humanoid machines made to serve humans' emotional needs).

That's just one of countless fictions (in film, TV, books, comics, etc.) positing sentient machines; some looking like humans, some not.

(My favorite evil-computer movie is still *Colossus: The Forbin Project* (1970). Future *Young and the Restless* star Eric Braeden plays a tech genius, hired to make a supercomputer to run the US nuclear arsenal. The computer (with a voice but not a "face") becomes sentient and decides that, as the only truly rational being, it deserves to control the world.)

Ray Kurzweil's *The Age of Spiritual Machines* (1999) and *The Singularity Is Near* (2005) claimed computers would not only "exceed human intelligence," but would become conscious, with free will and "emotional and spiritual experiences." His "singularity" is a future moment (perhaps by 2045) in which human and artificial intelligence will merge; *"and all disease, aging, social ills, and death will be reversed, resolved, or eliminated."*

Israeli author Yuval Noah Harari's *Homo Deus* (2015) "suggests that Homo sapiens may not be dominant in a universe where big data becomes a paradigm" (Wikipedia). Harari asks, "What will happen to society, politics, and daily life when non-conscious but highly intelligent algorithms know us better than we know ourselves?"

Harari was one of many in the mid 2010s who predicted that, by now (2025) or a few years after, artificial intelligence would become more intelligent than humans, and would even replace most lawyers (while "disrupting" many other professions, including medical diagnoses. Also, self-driving cars would ruin the auto (and auto insurance) industries).

While that great AI disruption hasn't happened yet, some folks still say it all (or much of it) will happen any year now. They claim we're close to getting "artificial general intelligence," the ability of machines to think like humans do. (Others claim that's still far off and may even be impossible).

(Note: Most of the illustrations in this book were either created or adapted with the help of AI image tools. I believe in using available tools to help humanity and self-expression, but not letting those tools "use" us.)

STARVING THE ROOTS TO FEED THE 'STEM'S

I believe computers will keep getting better at "crystallized intelligence." But for "fluid intelligence," the truly creative and human (and MISCous) kind of thinking: You'll still need people for that, and probably always will. It's our advantage, and we've gotta keep it.

In the last few pre-COVID years in schools, the whole of the national education industry had become ever-more obsessed with the singular cause of "STEM." Every student everywhere was supposed to be funneled into "Science, Technology, Engineering, and Math"—often thinly disguised jargon for wanting everybody to become a computer programmer, because that's where the only high-paying jobs were expected to be.

The Tree of Knowledge (in the educational, not the Biblical, term) is traditionally depicted with its underground roots growing just as bountifully as its above-ground blossoms and, yes, its stems.

Around the country, activist programs about helping girls and ethnic minorities in schools got "pivoted" toward funneling as many girls and ethnic minorities as possible into STEM.

In some places, "STEM" was revised into "STEAM" by adding "Arts" as a vestigial appendage.

But humanity does not live by STEM (or even by STEAM) alone.

We need more *bricoleurs*, not just more engineers.

We need more creators and care givers, not just more (corporate or military) soldiers.

We need to teach, and learn and maintain, more fluid intelligence (or, as I've called it here, MISCous thought).

THE MISCosity MANIFESTO

In another sense, the MISCous stance is similar to the stoics' notion of *amor fati*, of accepting and even loving your current moment and lot in life.

This is NOT simply "letting it be," or "going with the flow."

It's more like the old bumper sticker slogan, *"Bloom where you are planted."*

It's saying "Yes, I'm (Black, Latinx, immigrant/undocumented, indigenous, female, gay/lesbian/bi/trans/asexual, nerdy, introverted, physically disabled, economically downscale, etc. etc.) *and* I'm proud of it, *and* want a better life for myself and my loved ones and everybody else *because*, not in spite of, who I proudly am."

And, no matter what our ages or backgrounds, we need to learn and act and exist as parts of a more functional whole.

We need to learn to be part of a better world, a better "tribe," a better humanity.

Which, again, involves the issue of how to make a better human society.

It's perhaps THE big issue of our, or any, age.

Where do we go from here? And how do we get there?

As we hinted at a while back, we'll now try to imagine a future.

A future made up of infinite other futures, not just one.

World-building is what sci-fi/fantasy authors and video-game designers call the creation of a whole fictional biosphere of sorts, a "universe."

As authors and painters and animators have shown over the decades, one can imagine anything.

But, as the Oulipo people would say, "constraints" can actually free the imagination.

So: the world we'll imagine, and the means by which we imagine it, will have some constraints.

The first constraint we'll deal with here: a world subject to the same physical laws as ours. Gravity, carbon-based life forms, your basic human species with no mutant superpowers, etc.

The second constraint: a future society that used to be the one we've got in "real" life now, but which has since become significantly better for as many humans as possible.

In short, a utopia, more or less (at least opposite of a dystopia, of which we've had a vast surplus, both in fictional media and "real" life).

Not a society where everything's perfect forever (which, in a universe of constant change, can never be); but rather, a society that's optimally set up to successfully handle what problems come about.

Then (the third and most difficult constraint, as we've mentioned): imagine a (more or less) utopia that's (more or less) filled with people who aren't necessarily just like you—in ethnicity, gender, sexual preference, lifestyle, religion, etc.

As we've said, there are plenty of imagined future utopias (or imagined past golden ages) either dominated or solely occupied by people just like the person doing the imagining. Futures where everyone's a vegan, or a radical lesbian, or a technocrat, or a free-market Libertarian, or a gun-toting "survivalist," or an upper-middlebrow intellectual, or (or rather and, in almost all of the above scenarios) "white" (not that "white" really means a damn thing).

(Lyman Tower Sargent, quoted in the "Utopia" article on Wikipedia: "...There are socialist, capitalist, monarchical, democratic, anarchist, ecological, feminist, patriarchal, egalitarian, hierarchical, racist, left-wing, right-wing, reformist, naturist/nude Christian, free love, nuclear family, extended family, gay, lesbian, and many more utopias... Utopianism, many argue, is essential for the improvement of the human condition. But if used wrongly, it becomes dangerous. Utopia has an inherent contradictory nature here."

Similarly, most attempts to create a real-life utopia on earth have been based on the premise of a more or less homogeneous group conforming to a prescribed "system" of work, economics, sex/family life, etc.

As we've mentioned, they generally collapse or drift apart, no later than the second generation. Notions of "free love" collide into the existence of either jealousy or newly adolescent offspring; or the farm or artisanal factory goes broke; or a charismatic leader loses absolute control over his followers; or changing economic conditions collide with a "system" that's not built to evolve.

Some late 1800s-early 1900s communal movements were strictly agrarian. Others formed their own light- or heavy-industrial enterprises.

So instead, let's imagine a different kind of future.

What if large numbers of people (I'd never say everybody, because this isn't about conformity, not even about non-conformist conformity) were to apply the lessons of MISCosity?

Not heaven on earth.

But perhaps a place where the many short- and long-term problems humans will always have are more accurately diagnosed and more effectively addressed.

Where everybody knows everybody's weird, but they manage to (more or less) get along anyway.

Where the elements of humanity oscillate and vibrate and move just like the elements of nature.

Where all the problems still exist, but we're better able to address them together.

We're not making a singular new society, innately conformist as those attempts always are or eventually become.

No, we're on a much more challenging but more beneficial and viable project: a world that honors and nourishes all (well, most) of the loving weirdness that's already here.

(Sci-fi author N.K. Jemisin to the Paris Review*):"...I was trying to figure out what a society might be like if it was genuinely a good place, and I realized as I was trying to think of it—science-fiction writers are supposed to be able to come up with futures. All futures. But the one thing I could not imagine was a society stemming from our own that was truly inclusive, truly egalitarian, and truly good for all people. What a true utopian society was like."*

This is no mere academic exercise.

As Oscar Hammerstein II put it in the musical *South Pacific*, "If you don't have a dream, then how you gonna make a dream come true?"

Stephen Duncombe's 2007 book *Dream* (reissued as *Dream or Nightmare*) is about the need for progressive movements to offer a positive, attractive vision of a better future. Not just slowing down environmental damage, but making a healthier place for humans and other creatures to live. Not just fighting racism/sexism/homophobia, but celebrating people's differences and putting them to productive use in improving conditions for all.

The Black Lives Matter movement has taught many about Black liberation and survival movements in general, and how they've sustained themselves over the decades and centuries. Out of stark necessity, generation after generation of activists, scholars, and just plain folks have passed down the skills to do all you could to make the world around you more hospitable to you and yours, and to preserve your own health and sanity at the same time. Theirs was and is no mere youthful exercise in "revolutionary" hedonism, to be followed by a promised "happily ever after" life of domestic complacency. It's about wresting control of your own present, and hence your future (in both the French singular/informal *tu* and the collective/formal *vous* forms of "you").

IT WON'T BE EASY

How to get on the road to that future?

Start by encouraging/honoring the differentiations, the diversity beyond the white-upscale notion of "diversity" (i.e., more than just white-upscale men, white-upscale women, and white-upscale gays).

Think of a place, say, your own community and your own nation.

Notice, really notice (perhaps for the first time), all the ethnicities and genders and classes and "tribes" all around you, especially the ones you ignore or take for granted.

Imagine that they all, we all, have aching hearts and inquisitive minds, yearning souls and unmet dreams.

See the place where you live as a place where everybody's weird and nobody's superior.

And then imagine, in as much detail as possible, a place where all these freaks live more or less in harmony, AND how to establish that here on Earth.

And then work to make it real.

That, along with taking care of our loved ones and ourselves, is our task in this life.

Not amassing money or stuff.

Not having thrilling personal adventures.

Not achieving individual beauty, strength, or power.

But envisioning, and then making, a new world, a world (or society or culture or "scene") better suited to help everybody thrive together.

(Didn't say it would be easy.)

This, the meta-task (and "metta task") of humanity, involves, by necessity, rethinking every big and little societal institution.

The events of the year 2020-21 (including Black Lives Matter, the pandemic and its related shutdowns, and the attempted overthrow of the US government) encouraged more people to reconsider the whole race/gender/class caste system, to envision new institutions to replace some or all of local police departments' functions, to defend (or in the US, to build mostly from scratch) a robust public health care system, to rethink schools and entertainment and even work.

•

Parenting and schooling for a more MISCous world would emphasize the importance of a good (moral, ethical, and intellectual) "compass."

As we've learned about fluid intelligence, when minds/brains of any age (but particularly younger ages) are (or become) permeable, they can be more vulnerable to manipulation under false senses of certainty.

We want young *and* old people to question a lot of things. Especially the cultural premises that keep some people/peoples suppressed.

Boomer-centric "subversive education," predicated on keeping kids away from both formalized rote-learning and from (yes) television, isn't the approach for today.

Chris Sperry and Cyndy Scheibe, in *Teaching Students to Decode the World*, instead promote "constructivist media decoding." It's teaching "analysis of media materials—including print and digital documents, videos and films, social media posts, advertisements, and other formats—with an emphasis on critical thinking and collaboration." Getting kids to question, not blindly accept, what's in new, old, and "social" media.

TO MAKE IT SHORT... 154

But remember that certain things, as we've discussed on previous pages, should NOT be still matters of debate by now. Among them:

- We have to take care of the planet as our species' only available habitat.
- We have to take care of one another.
- Ego games, bigotry, and the addiction to abusive displays of "power" and false notions of "superiority" (including but not limited to "rape culture" and "white privilege") are incredibly stupid.
- Knowledge, no matter how incomplete (and it always will be), is preferable to ignorance.
- Information is different from (and better than) emotional manipulation.
- Hip nihilism never accomplished anything. This is something my (white) '80s-'90s generation got wrong.
- Information is different from (and better than) emotional manipulation.

And much more.

Also remember the way constructive (rather than destructive) change happens.

To make it short, you can't make it short.

A victory doesn't mean that everything is now going to be nice forever and we can therefore all go lounge around until the end of time.

Some activists are afraid that if we acknowledge or celebrate even a minor, partial "victory," people will give up the struggle.

I've long been more afraid that people will give up and go home—or never get started in the first place—if they think no victory is possible, or fail to recognize the victories already achieved. Marriage equality is not the end of homophobia, but it's still something major, something to celebrate. A victory is a milestone on the road, evidence that sometimes we win, and encouragement to keep going, not to stop.

You shouldn't look ahead to a single future "revolutionary event," just as you shouldn't fear a single future "apocalyptic event" (the premise of all those "post-apocalyptic" novels, graphic novels, films, TV series, etc.).

The "promised land," Heaven on Earth, Utopia, whatever you call it: It won't appear all at once. Nothing really good does.

There won't be a single moment where you'll be able to say it's "arrived." The future will always be a work in "progress" (in both senses of the term).

It will have setbacks (disputes, wars, reactionary movements).

(Rebecca Solnit, Hope in the Dark*):"Change is rarely straightforward... Sometimes it's as complex as chaos theory and as slow as evolution. Even things that seem to happen suddenly arise from deep roots in the past or from long-dormant seeds."*

And it won't be perfection.

Humanity is, by nature, imperfect and always will be.

There will still be disagreements and heated arguments. Hearts will still be broken by romantic/sexual complications, shifting attractions/loyalties, frustrated desires, and just plain human failings.

There will still be diseases, accidents, and "timely" and "untimely" deaths.

But in this notion of a better world, we'll generally become a lot better at handling the situations that arise, because we'll be more able to work on these together. We'll have the advantage of more, and more different, points of view to approach new individual and collective situations.

It will be largely because we (or at least enough of us) will realize that capital-B "Business" isn't everything.

In 1998, economist and Gandhian scholar Romesh Diwan introduced the concept of "relational wealth": *"Relational wealth emanates from our interconnections with other human beings. It gives us inner strength and emotional security and defines our quality of life. There is a tension between material and relational wealth. As material wealth increases beyond a certain level, it impinges on relational wealth.... Yet the objective of a meaningful economic practice and policy is to maximize material and relational wealth jointly."*

Umair Haque, a British-born neuroscientist and economic consultant, promotes the similar concept of "eudainomics." (The name comes from *eudaimonia*, a Greek term that can be translated to mean "happiness" or "human flourishing or prosperity.") As Haque puts it, it means a society that evolves *"...from one that single-mindedly, one-dimensionally maximizes near-term income, at the price of the well-being, health, flourishing, of you, me, our grandkids, and our planet, to one that elevates and expands all that."*

You've now learned, on a shallow but broad level, about our ultra-complex world, including our ultra-complex species.

About acknowledging this world as it now is, without giving up on making things better.

About adapting yourself to get along, and even thrive, within such a world.

About using stories and the arts to help train a more adaptive and creative mind.

About imagining a future where more people are more prosperous, more egalitarian, more accepted, and more attuned to the world's (and humanity's) complexities.

About learning, then taking, some of the many big and little steps needed to make such a future happen.

Now go out there and make a better world. A world more attuned to its complexities. A more MISCous world.

ENDNOTES

6: Rob Doyle, *Threshold*. Bloomsbury Publishing, 2020.
12: Megan Lim, "Why Chaos Is Our Greatest Love." medium.com/the-mission/why-chaos-is-our-greatest-love-292ad1cf3d4f
Carl Jung, *The Collected Works of C.G. Jung*, Volume 9 Part 1. Princeton University Press, 1969.
en.wikipedia.org/wiki/Chaos_theory
17: Richard Powers, *The Overstory*. W.W. Norton, 2018.
18: en.wikipedia.org/wiki/Homo_unius_libri
20: Francis Bacon, "Of Boldness." bartleby.com/lit-hub/reference/of-boldness/
The Spiritual Life, slife.org/absurdism/
21: Luigi Russolo, *The Art of Noises*. 1913-16. Cited at en.wikipedia.org/wiki/The_Art_of_Noises.
22: Douglas Hofstadter, *Gödel, Escher, Bach: an Eternal Golden Braid*. Basic Books, 1979.
Robert Shea & Robert Anton Wilson, *The Illuminatus! Trilogy*. Dell, 1975.
George Pendle, *Strange Angel: The Otherworldly Life of Rocket Scientist John Whiteside Parsons*. Mariner Books, 2006.
25: Timotheus Vermeulen & Robin van den Akker, "Notes on metamodernism." tandfonline.com/doi/full/10.3402/jac.v2i0.5677
Luke Turner, "The Metamodernist Manifesto," 2011. metamodernism.org
Jason Ananda Josephson Storm, *Metamodernism: The Future of Theory*. University of Chicago Press, 2021.
Greg Dember, *Say Hello to Metamodernism*. Exact Rush, 2024.
26: Simone Weil, *Gravity and Grace*. University of Nebraska Press, 1992.
27: en.wikipedia.org/Paradox; en.wikipedia.org/Zeno_of_Elea
"Paradox." literarydevices.net/paradox/
"Paradox." merriam-webster.com/dictionary/paradox
28: Michael Foucault, *This Is Not a Pipe*. University of California Press, 2008.
F. Scott Fitzgerald, "The Crack-Up." *Esquire*, February 1936.
29: Fritjof Capra, *The Tao of Physics*. Shambhala Publications, 1975.
30: "Jean-Paul Sartre's Concepts of Freedom & 'Existential Choice' Explained in an Animated Video Narrated by Stephen Fry." openculture.com/2018/02/jean-paul-sartres-concepts-of-freedom-existential-choice-explained-in-an-animated-video-narrated-by-stephen-fry.html
Simone de Beauvoir, *The Ethics of Ambiguity*. Philosophical Library, 1948.
Gary Cox, *How to Be an Existentialist: or How to Get Real, Get a Grip and Stop Making Excuses*. Continuum, 2011.
31: Tara Brach, *Radical Acceptance: Embracing Your Life With the Heart of a Buddha*. Bantam, 2004.
32: Alan W. Watts, *The Wisdom of Insecurity: A Message for an Age of Anxiety*. Vintage Books, 1951.
34: Rachel Carson, *Silent Spring*. Houghton Mifflin, 1962.
36: James Burke, *Connections 1*. BBC Video/Ambrose Video, 2007.
37: Julio Cortázar, *Hopscotch: A Novel*. Pantheon, 1967.
Jorge Luis Borges, *Labyrinths*. New Directions, 1962.
38: Vannevar Bush, "As We May Think." *The Atlantic*, July 1945.
Ted Nelson, *Computer Lib/Dream Machines*. Self-published, 1974; reissued by Tempus/Microsoft Press, 1987.
39: J.A. Ginsburg, jaginsburg.com
40: John Guare, *Six Degrees of Separation*. Knopf Doubleday, 1990.

Albert-László Barabási, *Linked: The New Science Of Networks*. Perseus, 2002.

Jorge Luis Borges, *A Universal History of Infamy*. E. P. Dutton, 1972.

41: Max Ophüls, director: *La Ronde*, 1950 film from Arthur Schnitzler play.

Robert D. Putnam, *Bowling Alone: The Collapse and Revival of American Community*. Simon & Schuster, 2000.

42: Johann Hari, *Lost Connections*. Bloomsbury USA, 2018.

Betty Friedan, *The Feminine Mystique*. W.W. Norton, 1963.

Laboria Cuboniks, *The Xenofeminist Manifesto: A Politics for Alienation*. Verso, 2018.

Krishnamurti Foundation, kfoundation.org/it-is-no-measure-of-health-to-be-well-adjusted-to-a-profoundly-sick-society/

43: Zat Rana, "Why You Are Not Who You Say You Are," 2018. Reposted at theladders.com/career-advice/you-are-not-who-you-say-you-are

45: Ursula K. LeGuin, *Words Are My Matter: Writings on Life and Books*. Harper Perennial, 2016.

50: George Woodbridge (art); anonymous (text), "How to Be a MAD Non-Conformist." *MAD* #49, June 1959.

51: Chimamanda Ngozi Adichie, "The danger of a single story." ted.com/talks/chimamanda_ngozi_adichie_the_danger_of_a_single_story

52: Gabor Maté, *In the Realm of Hungry Ghosts: Close Encounters with Addiction*. North Atlantic Books, 2010.

Sally Kohn, *The Opposite of Hate: A Field Guide to Repairing Our Humanity*. Algonquin Books, 2018.

Erin Vanderhoof, "Ijeoma Oluo and Aminatou Sow on Sally Kohn's Book and What Comes Next." vanityfair.com/style/2018/04/ijeoma-oluo-amintaou-sow-sally-kohn

54: Tim Wise, *Dear White America: Letter to a New Minority*. City Lights Publishers, 2012.

Jamil Zaki, *The War for Kindness: Building Empathy in a Fractured World*. Crown, 2019.

Steve Silberman, *NeuroTribes: The Legacy of Autism and the Future of Neurodiversity*. Avery, 2015.

55: Liane Kupferberg Carter, "Autism and Empathy," 2013. huffpost.com/entry/autism-and-empathy_b_3281691

57: Jennifer Peepas, jenniferpeepas.com

"Loving Your Enemies." kinginstitute.stanford.edu/king-papers/documents/loving-your-enemies

58: Joseph Brodsky, *Less Than One: Selected Essays*. Penguin Classics, 2011.

Hannah Arendt and Mary McCarthy, *Between Friends: The Correspondence of Hannah Arendt and Mary McCarthy*. Harcourt Brace, 1995. Excerpted at themarginalian.org/2016/06/21/mary-mccarthy-between-friends-evil/

59: John Steinbeck, *Steinbeck: A Life in Letters*. Viking, 1989. Excerpted at themarginalian.org/2016/12/30/john-steinbeck-new-year/

James Baldwin, *The Price of the Ticket: Collected Nonfiction, 1948-1985*. St. Martin's Press, 1985.

Paul Bloom, *Against Empathy: The Case for Rational Compassion*. Ecco Books, 2016.

60: Toni Morrison, *The Source of Self-Regard*. Knopf, 2019.

Karen Armstrong, *Twelve Steps to a Compassionate Life*. Knopf, 2010.

61: "Theory of Mind." psychologytoday.com/us/basics/theory-of-mind

ENDNOTES

Eric Kandel, "Theory of Mind: Why Art Evokes Empathy," 2013. bigthink.com/articles/theory-of-mind-why-art-evokes-empathy/

65: Angie Hodapp, "Kishotenketsu and Non-Western Story Structures," 2022. nelsonagency.com/2022/01/kishotenketsu-and-non-western-story-structures/

68: "The Hero's Journey and Joseph Campbell." jcf.org/learn/joseph-campbell-heros-journey

Anne Carson, *Eros the Bittersweet*. Princeton University Press, 1986.

82: Susan Sontag, *Against Interpretation*. Farrar, Straus and Giroux, 1966.

Jacques Derrida, *Basic Writings*. Routledge, 2007.

83: Jim Powell, *Postmodernism For Beginners*. For Beginners, 2007.

84: "Remodernism." en.wikipedia.org/wiki/Remodernism

Larry McCaffery, *Conversation with David Foster Wallace*. Dalkey Archive Press, 1993.

85: Gita Jackson, "The Video Games That Made People Question Their Beliefs," 2019. kotaku.com/the-video-games-that-made-people-question-their-beliefs-1836045401

90: Guy Debord, *Society of the Spectacle*. Black & Red, 1970.

David Foster Wallace, introduction to *The Best American Essays 2007*. Mariner Books, 2007.

91: Naomi Wolf, *The Beauty Myth: How Images of Beauty Are Used Against Women*. William Morrow & Co, 1991.

92: Ric Burns, director: *Andy Warhol: A Documentary Film*. PBS Video, 2006.

94: zinnedproject.org/materials/bread-and-roses-song/

95: Marshall McLuhan, Quentin Fiore, Jerome Agel: *The Medium is the Massage: An Inventory of Effects*. Bantam Books, 1967.

98: Zadie Smith, *On Beauty*. Hamish Hamilton, 2005.

Elaine Scarry, *On Beauty and Being Just*. Princeton University Press, 1999.

W. B. Yeats, *The Collected Poems of W.B. Yeats*. Scribner, 1996.

99: Milan Kundera, *The Unbearable Lightness of Being*. Harper & Row, 1984.

101: Philip Core, *Camp: The Lie That Tells the Truth*. Plexus Publishing, 1996.

102: Art Chantry, *Art Chantry Speaks: A Heretic's History of 20th Century Graphic Design*. Feral House, 2015.

104: Julie Peters, *WANT: 8 Steps to Recovering Desire, Passion, and Pleasure After Sexual Assault*. Turner Publishing, 2019.

105: Robyn Griggs Lawrence, *The Wabi-Sabi House: The Japanese Art of Imperfect Beauty*. Clarkson Potter, 2004.

106: Victor Segalen, *Essay on Exoticism: An Aesthetics of Diversity*. Duke University Press reprint, 2002.

108: Michael Harris, *The End of Absence: Reclaiming What We've Lost in a World of Constant Connection*. Current, 2014.

110: Thomas More, *Utopia*. fulltextarchive.com/book/Utopia/

Michael Caines, "Utopia: Nine of the most miserable attempts to create idealised societies." independent.co.uk/news/world/politics/utopia-nine-of-the-most-miserable-attempts-to-create-idealised-societies-a6887316.html

111: Edward Bellamy, *Looking Backward*. gutenberg.org/files/624/624-h/624-h.htm

Ernest Callenbach, *Ecotopia*. Bantam, 1977.

THE MISCosity MANIESTO

"*Things to Come*, the 1936 Sci-Fi Film Written by H.G. Wells, Accurately Predicts the World's Very Dark Future." openculture.com/2016/09/hg-wells-things-to-come.html

David Butler, director: *Just Imagine*, 1930. archive.org/details/just-imagine_1930

112: Michael Moorcock, "Starship Stormtroopers," 1977. libcom.org/article/starship-stormtroopers-michael-moorcock

113: Maggie McNeill, maggiemcneill.com/ 2016/08/12/ulro/

Susanna Andrews, thecollector.com/william-blake-mythology-4-states-of-mind/

Ellie Clayton, ramhornd.blogspot.com

114: "Ursula K. Le Guin," Library of America. loa.org/writers/655-ursula-k-le-guin/

"The Patternist Series." octaviabutler.com/patternist-series

Marge Piercy, *Woman on the Edge of Time*. Random House, 1976.

Aja Romano, "Hopepunk, the latest storytelling trend, is all about weaponized optimism." vox.com/2018/12/27/18137571/what-is-hopepunk-noblebright-grimdark

115: "Heaven Is A Place Where Nothing Ever Happens." studionathancoley.com/works/heaven-is-a-place-where-nothing-ever-happens-2

118: E.M. Forster, *The Machine Stops and Other Stories*. Moncrieffe, 2024.

119: "Technocracy movement." en.wikipedia.org/wiki/Technocracy_movement

Industrial Workers of the World, iww.org

"Charles Fourier." britannica.com/biography/Charles-Fourier

120: Murray Bookchin, *Post-Scarcity Anarchism*. Ramparts Press, 1971.

"Tech-Bros and Techno-Utopias." https://dartsandletters.ca/tech-bros-and-techno-utopias-a-darts-and-letters-mini-series/

"Blueseed." https://en.wikipedia.org/wiki/Blueseed

121: Jane Jacobs, *The Death and Life of Great American Cities*. Random House, 1961.

123: Greg Epstein, "So you want to talk about race in tech with Ijeoma Oluo." techcrunch.com/2020/06/13/so-you-want-to-talk-about-race-in-tech-with-ijeoma-oluo/

126: Nick Hanauer, "How to Destroy Neoliberalism: Kill 'Homo Economicus.'" evonomics.com/how-to-destroy-neoliberalism-kill-homo-economicus/

George F. Will. *The Leveling Wind: Politics, the Culture, and Other News, 1990-1994*, Penguin, 1995.

127: adrienne maree brown, *Emergent Strategy*. AK Press, 2017.

130: Mike A. Shapiro, "A source for the quotation 'You shall know the truth, and the truth shall make you odd.'" mikeashapiro.wordpress.com/2021/01/31/a-source-for-the-quotation-you-shall-know-the-truth-and-the-truth-shall-make-you-odd/

"27 Life Changing Lessons to Learn from Eckhart Tolle." thinkinghumanity.com/2015/02/27-life-changing-lessons-to-learn-from-eckhart-tolle.html

Herbert Marcuse, *Eros and Civilization: A Philosophical Inquiry into Freud*. Beacon Press, 1955.

Chip Richards, 2019, reposted at seattleaikikai.com/news/

131: Andrew Harvey, *The Hope: A Guide to Sacred Activism*. Hay House, 2009.

Lerita Coleman Brown, *What Makes You Come Alive: A Spiritual Walk with Howard Thurman*. Broadleaf, 2023.

ENDNOTES

Philippians 4:7.
133: Emily Dickinson, *Hope Is the Thing with Feathers: The Complete Poems of Emily Dickinson*. Gibbs Smith, 2019.
Og Mandino, *The Greatest Salesman in the World*. Bantam, 1968.
135: "Sane Insanity." theschooloflife.com/article/sane-insanity/
137: Ellen Forney, *Marbles: Mania, Depression, Michelangelo, and Me, A Graphic Memoir*. Gotham Books, 2012.
Ellen Forney, *Rock Steady: Brilliant Advice From My Bipolar Life*. Fantagraphics, 2018.
Mahita Gajanan: "Comedian Aparna Nancherla Is Everywhere Right Now. And She's Finding the Humor in Her Anxiety." time.com/5211530/aparna-nancherla-comedy-anxiety/
138: "David Foster Wallace: The 'Fresh Air' Interview," 1997. npr.org/2015/08/14/432161732/david-foster-wallace-the-fresh-air-interview
139: Scott Barry Kaufman, "Why Quieting the Ego Strengthens Your Best Self." scottbarrykaufman.com/quieting-ego-strengthens-best-self/
Paul Arden, *Whatever You Think Think The Opposite*. The Greatest Books, 2005.
141: Don Miguel Ruiz, *The Four Agreements*. Amber-Allen Publishing, 1997.
142: Ayesh Perera, "Fluid Intelligence vs. Crystallized Intelligence." simplypsychology.org/fluid-crystallized-intelligence.html
en.wikipedia.org/wiki/Fluid_and_crystallized_intelligence
143: Christopher Bergland, "Too Much Crystallized Thinking Lowers Fluid Intelligence." psychologytoday.com/us/blog/the-athletes-way/201312/too-much-crystallized-thinking-lowers-fluid-intelligence
Claude Lévi-Strauss, *The Savage Mind*. University Of Chicago Press, 1966.
144: René Ostberg, "Transhumanism." britannica.com/topic/transhumanism
Karel Čapek. "R.U.R.," 1920. gutenberg.org/files/59112/59112-h/59112-h.htm
145: Ray Kurzweil, *The Age of Spiritual Machines: When Computers Exceed Human Intelligence*. Viking, 1999.
Ray Kurzweil, *The Singularity Is Near*. Viking, 2005.
Yuval Noah Harari, *Homo Deus: A Brief History of Tomorrow*. Harper, 2017.
149: Lyman Tower Sargent, *Utopianism: A Very Short Introduction*. Oxford University Press, 2010.
150: Abigail Bereola, "A True Utopia: An Interview With N.K. Jemisin," 2018. theparisreview.org/blog/2018/12/03/a-true-utopia-an-interview-with-n-k-jemisin/
151: Stephen Duncombe, *Dream or Nightmare: Reimagining Politics in an Age of Fantasy*. O/R Books, 2007.
153: Chris Sperry and Cyndy Scheibe, *Teaching Students to Decode the World*. ASCD, 2022.
155: Rebecca Solnit, *Hope in the Dark: Untold Histories, Wild Possibilities*. Haymarket Books, 2016.
156: Romesh Diwan, "Relational wealth and the quality of life." sciencedirect.com/science/article/abs/pii/S1053535700000731?via%3Dihub
Umair Haque, "Eudaimonics: The Art of Realizing Genuinely Good Lives." medium.com/eudaimonia-co/eudaimonics-d55727be1233

Clark Humphrey's books include LOSER: The Real Seattle Music Story *(reissued by MISCmedia),* Walking Seattle *(from Adventure/ Keen), and* Vanishing Seattle *and* Seattle's Belltown *(both from Arcadia Publishing). He writes a daily email newsletter about the city, its growth, and its contradictions at miscmedia.com.*

20th ANNIVERSARY EDITION

LOSER
The Real Seattle Music Story

All the stars of the
'80s-'90s Seattle music scene
in one nerdishly-detailed book,
with hundreds of pictures.

It's back,
and it's louder than ever.

The interconnected origins and spectacular rise of

Nirvana • Pearl Jam • Hole
Soundgarden • Alice in Chains
Gas Huffer • Seven Year Bitch
Flop • The Supersuckers
Sir Mix-A-Lot • TAD • Fastbacks
Built to Spill • Bikini Kill
Sky Cries Mary • The Posies
Screaming Trees • Mudhoney
The Young Fresh Fellows • Beat Happening
The Presidents of the United States of America

How a subculture of self-proclaimed "losers"
became the darlings of the record industry,
only to get tossed aside like an old grungy shirt.

Now with even more pictures and stories,
an updated discography, and "whatever became of..." listings.

LOSER is the most complete account
of a phenomenon that rocked the world.

274 Big Pages • Over 900 Illustrations
Designed by the famed Art Chantry

Available from Amazon, CreateSpace, IngramSpark,
and direct at MISCmedia.com.

the ERRATICA FICTION series, #1:

the MYRTLE of VENUS

BETTY BEIGE, the world's blandest woman, inherits an old warehouse. She tries to evict its tenants, a ragtag group of underground artists. They decide to fight back. They'll win her over to their side. They'll use the power of seduction to make her an aware, sensual woman. Without knowing what's happening, Betty will turn from mild to wild.

Or will she?

That's just the start of the action, as eleven vivid characters cope with liberation, manipulation, high ideals, and lowdown-dirty deals. THE MYRTLE OF VENUS is a raucous, robust FUN novel, filled with:

- KINKY SEX! ORDINARY SEX!
- ART! MUSIC! DANCE! VIDEO GAMES!
- BURLESQUE DANCERS! FETISH PERFORMANCE ART!
- CIGARETTES! ALCOHOL! COFFEE! APHRODISIAC WATER!
- URBAN POLITICS! CLASS STRUGGLE!
- GREEK MYTHOLOGY! OUTER-SPACE CARTOONS!
- AN EXECUTIVE DOMINATRIX AND HER OFFICE BOY-TOYS!
- A WHITE GUY WHO WANTS TO BE A BLACK LESBIAN!
- A TALK-RADIO BAD BOY WITH CONTROL ISSUES!
- 'YOUNG, EDGY' ADVERTISING!
- SCHEMING WOMEN! NERDY MEN!
- A NAKED DRAG QUEEN!
- THE SECRET BEHIND AN AMERICAN ICON!

… and MUCH, MUCH MORE!

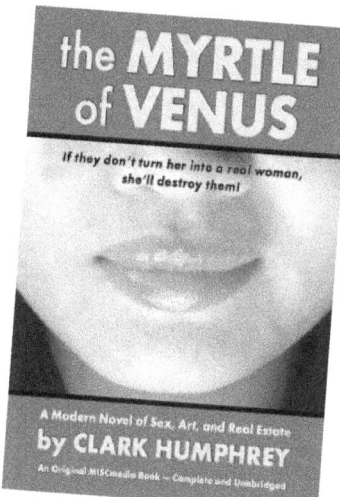

Available in print and ebook versions from Amazon, CreateSpace, and direct at MISCmedia.com.

the ERRATICA FICTION series, #2:

WHO AM I? WHY AM I HERE?

A clean-cut, seemingly ordinary teenage boy is on the run.
He just wants to get back to his suburban family.
But so many different people want him:

- As a centerpiece of occult rituals.
- As a model patient for an experimental healing therapy.
- As a nature boy.
- As a sex toy.

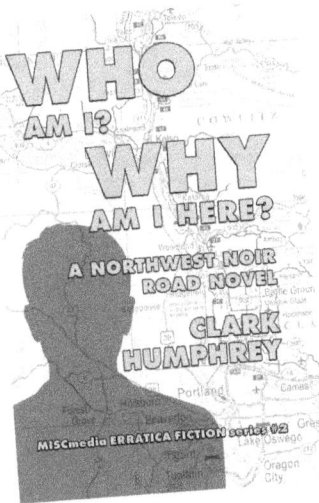

Along his journey, he meets many friends and/or enemies (he isn't always sure which is which).

As he goes from one danger to the next, the boy learns things he'd never known about himself, his past, and his hidden ability to end the world as we know it.

(Confused by all this? So is he!)

Available in print and ebook versions
from Amazon, CreateSpace,
and direct at MISCmedia.com.

From Seattle's historic Columbia City: Experiments in short-form fiction, in a wide array of styles, settings, and genres.

Organized by Elaine Bonow.

Stories from:

Daphne Bellflower
Elaine Bonow
Ren Felman
Dalmatia Fleming
Tom Gaffney
Clark Humphrey
Joanne Klein
Captain Sunderland

Available from Amazon and CreateSpace.

• JUSTICE • WEATHER • SPORTS • ZONING • TRANSIT • LABOR •

YOUR NEW SEATTLE NEWS DIGEST
CLARK HUMPHREY'S

BRIGHT, BRISK, BREEZY
PHONE-FRIENDLY DESIGN
IN YOUR E-MAIL BOX
EACH WEEKDAY MORNING

SIGN UP TODAY AT

MISCMEDIA.COM/MAIL

• PLANNING • POLITICS • CULTURE • ARTS • ECO • BIZ • ACTIVISM •

www.ingramcontent.com/pod-product-compliance
Lightning Source LLC
Chambersburg PA
CBHW070102080526
44586CB00013B/1165